LIFE AND TIMES OF
A MIDDLE EAST OIL MAN

PETER A, OLDHAM

Copyright ©2023 *PETER A, OLDHAM*

All Rights Reserved

Disclosure

The content presented in this book is based on the author's personal perspective and experiences. It is important to understand that the information provided within these pages should not be considered as exact facts or universal truths. The author's viewpoints, interpretations, and opinions shape the narrative of this book. Readers are encouraged to approach the content with an open mind and critical thinking. The publisher does not guarantee the accuracy, completeness, or reliability of the information presented. Each reader's understanding and interpretation may differ. It is advisable to supplement this book with additional sources and perspectives to gain a comprehensive understanding of the subject matter.

Dedication

This is to the ex-pats and specifically addressed to those of you who have worked in various remote desert locations, sacrificing precious time with your families, missing out on the significant developmental stages of your children's growth and the unwavering support of your wives, without whom your success may not have been possible.

Please remember to keep your spirits high and stay motivated, as you continue to overcome obstacles and face challenges head-on. Keep the wind on your back and your powder dry, as you navigate through the journey ahead.

Acknowledgements

I am deeply grateful to my amazing wife, Susan, who lovingly raised my children while I was embracing the joys of life. Without her unwavering support, I would not have had the opportunity to pen this book. Furthermore, I am incredibly blessed to have four lovely grandchildren who bring immense joy to our lives.

Thank you, Susan, for everything.

About The Author

Peter A. Oldham was born at Aspland Maternity in a small village called Gee Cross in 1954. He started his schooling at Holy Trinity School in the village, but left there at the bottom of his year. He then attended Greenfield Secondary School where he left at the age of 16, bottom of his class. Despite being told that he would never amount to anything and only have menial jobs for the rest of his working life, he had a dream and pursued it relentlessly.

Peter believes that one should never work for someone else's dream and that everyone is a star child of the universe who can and will achieve their dreams. He encourages readers to stand outside a barber shop long enough, and they will get a free haircut. Peter has had a rollercoaster of a life, having seen and done more in one year than the average person does in a lifetime. He finished up with four houses, a nice pension, three great kids, a good wife, two golden retrievers, money in the bank, and a motorhome, all because he had that dream.

Peter encourages readers to read his book and live their dream lives.

It's not over till you say it's over

And it's not over till you win

You are more powerful than you ever think you are

Don't stop running from your dream

Someone's opinion about you does not have to be your reality

CHEATING THE START

When I left school, I left with no education, but I had a dream, and it was not what my mother and father wanted. Always do what your heart tells you. They got me an apprenticeship at a firm in Hyde called C.A. Hardens as a centre lathe turner; having not a fucking clue what was one of those, the company sent me to college for one year to get some knowledge of what they wanted me to do for the rest of my life. As you will find out, I had other ideas, so I left school in July at 16 and started work. During my first three months at college, which started in August, I found the experience to be a complete joke and genuinely disliked it.

No interest in studying and only in fishing. Nothing really happened for the 12 months at college, only that I started to mix with people who really did not give a fuck about college. I at least had to try passing college, or I would be in the cotton mills on fuck all.

The day I left, they gave me all the tools I made over the year at college. They were not worth a wank. Basically, they did not work, and these tools went straight into the bin when I arrived home.

I soon realized that I was only spending one day a week at college while working four days a week, which didn't suit me. In response, I began writing "PAO" on the walls. It took three years for someone to discover that I was responsible for the graffiti, and I was brought before the board. They told me to either stop or they would inform my employer. At that point, I had just received my city and guilds certification, so I decided to quit and never return. I was a bit of a rebel at the time, not interested in going with the flow. As the saying goes, it's better to live 10 years as a wolf than 59 years as a sheep.

A year later, I started working at a factory, with only a little more experience than when I had first started out. At first, I felt like I fitted in with the other 40 centre lathe turners, all of whom smoked Park

Drive cigarettes. Soon enough, I started smoking 20 cigarettes a day myself.

It was not long, maybe 4 months when I got my feet under the carpet. I realised this was not me. During my shifts at work, I would often glance out the window onto Dowson Rd, where a number 30 bus would pass by. In fact, 25 buses would pass by during my shift. The thought of spending 50 years doing the same thing day in and day out didn't sit well with me. I felt like I needed to get out of there. However, over time, I noticed that I was producing a lot of scrap material, much of which ended up in the reservoir behind my house. This gave me pause and made me reconsider my options.

I find it amusing that 24 years after my time working at Hardens, the reservoir was drained, and I discovered many of the job items I had worked on, along with other items from various places I had worked as a centre lathe turner, were sticking out of the mud at odd angles. I also used to play a game where I would see how far I could throw 78 records, and some of them ended up quite far from where I had taken them from my house's wall.

Getting back to where we were. I was mixing with the wrong people who were very militant and would strike for anything. They did not want to sack me, but with the scrap or material that used to go missing and me being a time waster, I even set the record for stopping in the toilet, which was 2 hrs, and I broke that by one hour. I was still there because of the money they had invested in and hoping that I would improve over the years.

How I used to get the scrap work out of the factory. What I used to do was put the finished job on the floor, and the charge hand, who was a first-class cunt would pick them up and take them to the inspection table for passing off. When I knew one would be rejected, I would wait till dinner time when I knew the inspection team would be out for dinner and sneak in, put it into my bag ready for throwing into the reservoir, and I would take it back home. It could be a few months before they needed that part, so it all got lost in the great sea of things.

I worked at C.A. Hardens until I was 18 years old and spent around three years there. However, I never fitted in with their way of the matrix as I was a rebel and did not conform to society, i.e., Going home watching T.V. spending all your money at weekends and having to go back on Monday to earn some more. But what I did find out about the company was that there were people who travelled the world installing their equipment. This set a spark, but there will be a few years before I found my vocation.

I left there and got a job at Spark Engineering, which was a bad move; I got a job as a centre lathe turner. The boss was a Polish cripple who was a cunt; he wanted 8 hrs of work off you. On the second day he said to speed up the machine, which I did, and it was not fast enough, so he hobbled over on his crutches and put it on top speed.

The lathe was not bedded into the floor, so when it started to cut, the lathe started to bounce about, and yes, the job was scrapped. He just hobbled off and said get on with the rest. He whistled for me to come to him. I slowly walked over to him and said I am not a fucking dog; I am putting a week's notice in. At that time, you could just get a job anywhere. Engineering was taking off big time.

I then went to a pump manufacturer in Hyde. Bad move again. This was precision engineering, and my turning skills were not up to it plus, I had a dream of travelling and making money; many jobs there went into the reservoir at the back of my house. When asked where is it? I would just look stupid and just shrugged my shoulders, but about this time, the lads who I was drinking with were talking about cycling.

It came to a head when I was in the workshop about traveling the world. This struck me as a way of getting out of this working as a centre lathe turner which I hated plus, the turners were boring. I now look back, and they are still the same now boring fuckers, who have a shag once a week and under the thumb. Not for me, I thought. So it came to pass that I decided with one other guy to cycle around the world. The rest of the crowd thought it was nigh impossible. So I went to Eddy Merks in Manchester and got myself a second-hand bike with 4 panniers, 2 for the front and 2 for the back.

So Webby and I started to train every day throughout winter. We made a pact that we would set off on the 1st May after about a month of training and just getting my arse right with being in the saddle every day. I thought this was going to be hard and expensive. That was the seed of the dot that came to pass 5 days into the adventure. The great day came. We cheated at first. We caught a train to London then, cycled to Paddington, got a train to Dover, then sailed to France. All in one day, we were now in France. By this time, it was getting evening in Calais, and we decided to get out of town and find a place to camp. We got out of town about 4 miles when we saw what we thought was an abandoned quarry.

We got our shit together, made camp and a fire. On our first night in France, I took over a load of packet soup, enough for a week. We had water, so it was soup for tea. We got our heads down pretty early, and it was a good job. Around 5 am, there was such a noise I did not know what the fuck it was and neither did webby. We got out of the tent only to see truck after truck going into this quarry. It was a working quarry. Our bikes nearly got run over. Dust everywhere; we dismantled the camp, and off we tootled down the road.

A RESERVOIR OF SECRETS

We are all in the gutter, but some of us are looking at the stars

We were now heading down to Paris on our first full day of cycling; at around noon, we stopped at this little village whose name was forgotten in time for some cheese bread and water to get us to the next stop for the night, which would be on the outskirts of Paris.

This was when I started to realise this was not for me. I wanted to earn money, not spend it, but we cycled up and down dale under the trees that lined the roads.

My mind went to the second world war and how my dad might have come this way, heading for Dunkirk with the Germans coming up from the rear under the shade of these trees. He did tell me later in life it was around there where he left his second Vickers machine gun. He fired it for a full 10 hrs but had to leave it to make his escape to Dunkirk, where he was one of the very last to escape. He told me through the films, you see all the men in a file, getting on to boats to take you to the big ships out at sea. When he got there, it was everyone for himself; survival mode kicked in and later on, I had a few myself. The ship he got on was H.M.S Anthony which is my second name, but how he got to the boat is a book in itself, sadly, now lost in the sands of time, getting back to where we were.

We cycled for a full 10hrs till we got to a large lake. We thought this would be a great place to camp before riding into Paris. Same crack as the night before, set up camp, locked the bikes up, lit a fire and shoot the shit. Till around 10 pm got our heads down only to be awoken by the gendarmes at four in the morning; not speaking French, we knew what they meant. Fuck off. No camping here, so we hit the road. And up the road stopped to have breakfast and a wash from a little stream and for me, a fucking good shite which I had not had for three days washed my arse in the stream which was a bit sore with all this riding which we have been doing only another 20,0000 miles to go.

We hit Paris around 8 am, we wanted to see the burning flame and pay our respect to the unknown soldier who is buried there. So we decided to cross the roundabout. As you are well aware, it's 5 lanes. You try and take a bike across there. Fuck me, it nearly took me out twice, but we gave our respect, and off we rode down the Champs-Elysees; we had a coffee there just to say we had; by this time, I had enough of this. It was not for me, so we spent that night outside Paris.

This night was me trying to find a way of bailing out. I prayed. I did everything but sleep that night, but as night came to day, I thought if I don't do something, it's going to be harder than ever to get back home. Remember, I was just 20 and had never been abroad. Very naïve about things, so we continued and cycled past Orlay Airport. That's when I knew if I went much further, this would be my last chance to get home for a while. As we progressed past Orlay Airport, I started to pray very hard. I wanted to go home by the Airport.

This is when things take a turn for the best, We got to the top of the hill, and when we started to go down it, I noticed that once we hit bottom, we would have to really pedal to get up the next hill. So I got in a high gear at the bottom and started to power up the hill when all at once my pedals just started to just spin. When we got the bike stripped down we found that the spline that holds the two pedals together was in two pieces. This round bar was a inch thick. How on earth did that snap. I found out it had never been known before, people said faulty steel, but I know It was from above, I am sure. So, we are now in the shit. I said well, that's it; I am off, but we did go to a bike shop which was in the town about a mile away.

The problem was they had no spares because my shaft was imperial, and we were in France metric. So, after a little argument, to say the least, we departed. He went his way, and I went my way back to the Airport. Sold the bike, which paid for my flight back to London. I spent 2 days in London to make it a week away on the piss for 2 days, wondering if my name would be shit when they find out I left him out there, and yes, it was, but I was now thinking about what to do to get where I want to be which really, I did not know what that would be.

> Well, Mother was glad to see me. She got me a job in our street as a center lathe turner once again. It really did not rock my boat, but I was getting a bit better at fitting the pieces I had turned. About 4 months later, I heard my mate was in a Kubutz in Israel and having a whale of a time, it was time for me to do some thinking.

"Even a stopped clock is right twice every day. After some years, it can boast of a long series of successes."

He was picking grapes one day and oranges the next mmm. I thought that was a nice lifestyle but was still not highly convinced that it was for me, but hey fuck it? I did not tell anyone till I was ready. It was around October when I told Mum and Dad they went bonkers. The lads said you go for it by this time, getting pissed off going to the pub listening to the same old shit doing the same old things clubbing at the weekend, and skint by Monday; So I bought an air ticket which lasted me 6 months Thought that should do.

Went from Manchester to London and flew ELAL to Telavi. Nothing happened on the plane, so now I have landed in Telavi at night, got my rucksack and then a taxi for what I thought one night, then off to the Kibbutz, but that was going to change big style; I told the taxi driver I needed a cheap place for the night well he took me to this hostel paid my money and shown a room with about 10 beds in find a fresh bed, and that's yours for the night knackered.

Well I walked down in between the beds, some unmade, some smelt of dried piss, so anyhow, I found a bed do not know what time it was, but I was bollocks. Found where the washroom was. I had a wash and got my head down. About one hour had gone by, and people started to come back, and that lasted until the early morning.

Then around 7 am, there was a bell to get up and have breakfast. Then on your way, I did, and now I was looking for the office in Telavi to book a Kibbutz. I was asking around till someone spoke English and told me where it was, and it was only a mile away? As I got there, it seemed to be closed. It was Shabbat there, Sunday, which is a Friday. Fuck me, I thought; what am I going to do for a full day here? I decided to find somewhere different to stay and spend the day at the beach if I knew where it was. I decided to spend the day on the beach and find a place to stop later in the day. I found the beach got a deck chair, tied my rucksack to the chair and put my shorts on, which were cut-down trousers that just looked like a tramp, really. On leaving Gee Cross, the landlord gave me a watch for my 21st birthday. It was engraved at the back. I treasured it, so I did not put it into my rucksack in case someone robbed it, so I went swimming with it on. Bad move. However, I noticed a lot of people with guns, and I mean plenty, but I still did not grasp that all the Arab countries hated them. There were many bombings in the country, and they just had a hostage rescue mission, operation Entebbe or operation Thunderbolt was a successful counterterrorist hostage rescue mission carried out by commandoes of the Israel Defence Force at Entebbe Airport in Uganda on 4 July 1976, 102 of 106 hostages rescued.

Peace comes from within Do not seek it without

Coming off the beach late afternoon, I noticed my watch had stopped working. Shit, I thought, but let's find somewhere to stop the night. I remember seeing a rundown-type hotel a few blocks down the road. So I made a hasty decision and got myself a room for the night. The first hour, I was looking at my new watch when I started to notice it was wet on the inside so I put it in the sun to dry out.

This did not work. Then I got this idea, it's full of salt, and if I took the back off and put it under the sink, it would flush out the salt. No, wrong move. I got my survival knife out and managed to take the back off and flush it out under the tap. Wrong move again. Yes, overnight, it went red and rusty. I then threw it in the bin. So, I found out it was just a cheap old watch, but the thought was there.

By this time, it was around 8 pm, time for a drink. Bad move. I went downstairs and got a table and got a beer. After drinking it, I ordered another. The barman said, "You should go downstairs; it's better," so like a sheep, I went downstairs. There was no one there, only three ladies at the bar. I found a seat, and just as I was going to sit down, one of the girls said, "Come sit up here with us." So, thinking fucking hell, this is great, I sat on a bar stool in the middle of two of them. When one got hold of my leg, the other was whispering sweet nothing in my ear. Then a bottle of champagne came with four glasses, then came 20 cigarettes with another bottle of cheap champagne.

After one hour, I said, "Who is paying for this?" "You are blondie," said the blond. "I only have a few shackles." Then they got up and went to different clients where this big bruiser came up and said, "You have 280 pounds in the hotel safe." He got hold of me and took me to the safe, and took my money out and took 200 pounds. This was a fucking great leveller. I went back to my room and took stock of what the fuck happened. I was a bit naive, to say the least. Well, after last year's disaster, I could not go home early. It would be the laughing stock. So, I decided I would try and find a kibbutz near Tela Viv, so I would not have to pay to travel.

The next morning, with no watch, I travelled to the office. I told them what had happened. They found room in a kubutz in a place called Rohaverk, which was around 20 miles out of Tel Aviv. When I got there, they put me in a hut with some posh Danish lad. Did not like the twat from the outset, but hay o got my shit together. I was introduced to the volunteers and was given a mother and father to look after me and go for dinner once a week. The first day, I was making new friends but seeing some of them, they took a dislike to me. Maybe I was on the defensive all the time. Well on a Friday everyone used to go back and see the sites. I could not because no money, so one week I told everyone let us have a party rather than go somewhere on Fridays we had it in my room bad move great night finished up with this ugly French woman. By fuck was she ugly.

Anyhow, to cut a long story short, a company came on-site to put up greenhouses. I got pally with one of the lads, who was a Brit, and asked him if he could find me a job with the company. So, I got the job but wouldn't start until after Christmas. I decided to go home for Christmas and go back to start the job in the New Year, which involved working all over the country.

After three months of picking oranges and bananas, there was a story about that. When picking bananas, I used to be teamed up with this burly Argentinian.

He was a resident there who used to teach me how to pick bananas with a machete. It was the burly Argentinian who showed me how to do it. One person would hit the base of the tree once, while the other would get the bunch of bananas and place them on his shoulder. Then, I would cut the bananas off the tree, and the other person would walk with them to the truck. Did you know that bananas are green when they are picked? One day, it was my turn to cut the bananas off the tree. I got a bit cocky and tried to speed up the job, but I missed the banana and took a piece of the Argentinian's nose off. He chased me all over for an hour, and that was the end of my banana-picking days. After that, they had me driving a tractor. I turned it over and nearly crushed myself. That was the end of that job. One great thing I did see there was a thunderstorm that dropped all the avocados. We all went out and picked them up, and they went to the poor people in the villages.

So, I got the job putting up greenhouses all over Israel. This is what I was looking for - working abroad for money. I told them I was going home for Christmas and coming back. Before I left, I wanted the lad who I shared with (he was a first-class knob) to be gone for good at Christmas, so I wouldn't have to meet him when I returned. But fate was not going to have this.

I came home and had a Christmas anti-climax. But on New Year's Eve, I was in the pub dancing on a table when I fell off and ended up in the hospital with a dislocated shoulder. That put an end to going back to Israel. But everything happens for a reason.

After 5 weeks on the sick, I found a job in Denton. It was on a capstan lathe, and I was not the best person for the job, but I started anyway. After the first week, I knew this was not for me. I was just looking forward to the weekend.

Clubbing all over Manchester, but still not finding what I wanted. Then I found out that three people from the same family went on a course in London for George Wimpy Worldwide in industrial radiography and are now in Saudi. I went around and saw one of the lads, and he gave me the rundown for the job and what to say at the interview. I sent off for the job, got an interview, and as a welder, got the job. The job entailed me going on a course for three months down in London at a place called Hayes, which is not very far from the airport. I had to get digs somewhere near. I did find some with an old couple who would now be long gone. So, my adventure starts once again. I had an old Hillman Hunter and one tape of Johnny Cash, and off I went one Sunday afternoon to my digs and started the course on Monday.

YOU ONLY LOSE WHAT YOU CLING TO

I arrived at my accommodation around 7 pm, spent an hour introducing myself, and then headed off to the pub. Londoners can be a strange breed, but as I read through this problem full of ethnics in Hayes, I ordered a pint of London Pride which was shit. Unfortunately, when I tried to strike up a conversation with some of the locals, they just ignored me. So, I had four pints and fucked off to my room to wait for the course to start in the morning.

The next day, I was one of the first to arrive and met the teacher, who seemed like a bit of a dick. As it turned out, he was exactly that. When everyone else arrived, 70 percent of the group came from London, while the rest were scattered across the length and breadth of England. I found that the Londoners were not very friendly, and the biggest knob of them all was the stepson of Steve Reed, the comedian.

The course started, and I knew I was over my depth again, so I became silent, which has stud me in very well over the years. You cannot drop yourself in it if you don't say anything. You see, I was not a welder. Everyone else was. Every week we had a test, and you had to get 70 percent first week just scraped through, so that was the first week I palled up with a Jordy, who was a bit rough to say the least. We used to get pissed most nights. One night, we went into London and missed the last tube. Hence, no more. He stole a car, and we drove back to our digs; there was another lad who was from Cardiff. He was a right know-all and kept coming first every week. My mate and I kept coming joint last for one month. After the first month, we were told if we didn't improve, we would be kicked off the course. So that night, we discussed what we were going to do. We found out that all the last course's test papers were stored in a cupboard. We then planned to break in and take the papers. We knew where the key was. No alarms, so the next night, half pissed, we got in and got 2 of the best papers on the course. No one knew, so the following Friday, we got 80 percent of the answers right compared to everyone else.

However, as they say, everything happens for a reason. The Cockneys were not pleased, as they thought those "northern bastards" would be sent home. So, for the rest of the course, we kept things low-key and managed to get a passing grade of 70 percent or slightly above.

However, on the last test, before leaving to wait for our deployment to Saudi Arabia, we both scored 100 percent. We gave the Cockneys the finger and told the Welsh twat that things would be different out there. It's a man's world, and that proved to be true. That course taught me that bullshit baffles brains, and you have to go the extra mile than the average Joe to get what you want.

While waiting for my deployment to Saudi Arabia, I met my future wife, Susan, at a place called Rotters in Manchester. It was a Friday night, and as usual, I was half-pissed. My chat line was that I was a helicopter pilot in Saudi Arabia. It was a bad call, as Susan actually worked with my dad. She told him on Monday that she had met his son, the helicopter pilot. My dad was not pleased that I had lied to such a lovely girl like Susan. Oh well, you have got to be in it to win it eventually, we started to court each other.

It took two months for me to get a slot time to fly out to Saudi Arabia, but the time had finally come. The place I was going to was Abqaiq.

About Abqaiq

Abqaiq is a gated community owned by Saudi Aramco. It is an oil processing facility located in the Eastern Province of Saudi Arabia, situated in the desert 60km southwest of the Dammam-Khobar metropolitan area and north of the Rub al-Khali, the second largest sand desert in the world, known as the "Empty Quarter". The community was built in the 1940s by Aramco, now Saudi Aramco.

When I was there, we lived in a camp just outside the main facility in long dorms that housed over 60 men. The buildings had toilets and showers in the middle, and there were around 50 of these barracks-style accommodations with a large swimming pool. It took me three hours to get into the country when I first arrived in Saudi Arabia, and it is still a time-consuming process to get through the airport. There was no alcohol allowed, and at the time, clothing from Marks and Spencer was not permitted.

One point worth mentioning is that I had to get a new passport because I had been in Israel on a Kibbutz. The customs inspections were strict, with baggage searches primarily for alcohol and any newspapers, magazines, or books with suggestive pictures or any mention of Israel. These inspections sometimes delayed arriving passengers for over two hours.

There were three of us on the plane going to the same place, Abqaiq. We got onto a bus and were taken to Dammam, the HQ of Wimpey. Passports were taken from us and we were given temporary cards until we got our Agar Mer, which we had to be carry at all times. Otherwise, we would go to jail.

First, we got a two-hour talk about dos and don'ts. Fuck me; you could go to prison for the slightest thing. Then they talked about drinking. Everyone drinks, but don't get caught and don't drink outside camp. That came back to me a few months down the line. In the afternoon, we got taken to the main garage and were given a Chevy truck each. They had the biggest tyres I had ever seen. We were told about the Abqaiq highway, which had more accidents than any other road in the world. Fuck me; the road was full of burnt-up trucks, lorries, etc. 60 clicks down the road; we came to the contractors' camp, where thousands of men from different countries worked for contracting companies supporting Aramco. There were Americans, Canadians, and Brits. There were also workers from Thailand, the Philippines, and Egypt, but there were few Saudi workers. It was too much like hard work for them.

The first day on camp was a talk on booze things to do and not do , as with drugs there is prohibition on the manufacture, sale possession and consumption of alcohol in Saudi Arabia, Drinking is punishable by public flogging, fines, or lengthy imprisonment, accompanied by deportation in certain cases trading in alcohol naturally carries a higher sentence with harsher punishment for anyone caught selling to Saudi nationals you may be arrested of smelling of booze when you come off your flight. The spirit we drank had the name Siddique meaning my friend. I will get into more details of the brewing of alcohol later in the book.

The first day on site was dedicated to getting my ID and attending safety talks on the plant's standards. During lunchtime, I would go back to my room, have lunch, go to the pool, and then back to work. On the first night, I did nothing but sleep, as I was experiencing travel fatigue and first-day blues. The next day, I met my boss, who was the superintendent of the boilers on the plant. Our job was to inspect them, more inspection than radiography, which was a good thing for me.

The first two weeks were pretty dull, but there was a market called the souk on the other side of the road that sold radios and cheap cassettes. Over the months, I bought a lot of cassettes, most of which were country and western music. After the second week, I started to drink alcohol, which was available, and we had parties in each of our rooms. However, one night things got out of hand. I said something that was total bull shit, and the guy I said it to took umbrage and tried to headbutt me. He missed my nose and hit my two front teeth, which embedded in his head. We then started to fight on the floor until we got separated. We went back to our rooms and slept it off. We made up the next day; he had a gash in his head, and I had two broken teeth. He was flying home in two days, having spent a year out there, and was due for his bonus. I could have stopped that, but I said nothing.

One day later, after getting the alcohol out of my system, I went to the doctor. He gave me a shot of penicillin, which was a bad move. I went back to my room, and suddenly, everything started spinning, and my legs, arm, and head began to swell up. Then I felt sick and was in a right old state. I got out of my room, collapsed on the floor, and the next thing I knew, I was in the hospital with a drip on me and feeling terrible. On the second day, they were now injecting me every few hours with something I did not know, but I knew I was not getting any better. On the third day, they had put so many injections into my arms that they started going into the top of my hands. Four days later, they couldn't do anything more for me, so they put me in an ambulance and sent me to Dhahran main hospital.

About Dhahran in the 70s

The main compound of the Arabian American Oil Company (Aramco), which also served as the residential area for the expatriate engineers, executives, and their families, was surrounded by a fence and could only be entered through locked, secured gates. It was a completely autonomous city with its own recreation facilities, clubs, swimming pools, bowling alleys, cinemas, schools, and supermarkets. Here, women were able to live a normal life, drive a car, and even wear shorts, as long as they stayed within the 4-square-mile enclosure. There was no alcohol of any kind, although clandestine stills were operated on site and in homes.

But the hospital I was going to was a cheap Arabic hospital because my firm would not pay for the best treatment for me, tossers. So, I was in this hospital 4th class. The journey down was not good; I was sick all the way there. They left me in a wheelchair for 2 hours waiting for a bed, and I was just spewing up all the time with no one coming to clean it. Fucking shite. They got me into a bed, and after tests on the first day, they found out that I was allergic to penicillin. So they started giving me treatment. After 2 days in this shit hole, they let me go, but it was not finished there. When they discharged me, I had no pants or shoes and little money. However, when I left to go down to Dammam, I was given a phone number for my company to pick me up. I did not know at the time that there were only 4 lines across to Al. khobar where the main office was. I spent 7 hours waiting to get a line and had no pants or shoes, looking like a right paraffin lamp with only a t-shirt, underpants, and 2 broken front teeth. At last, I got a lift back to camp and spent the following day by the pool. The next day, I got a job in the desert on a pipeline with a mate of mine.

We arrived on site and saw a truck parked near the pipeline. Two men were sitting down smoking. We approached them slowly, and as we walked alongside the pipeline, I noticed a radiographic strip wrapped around one of the welded joints. We stopped in our tracks and said, "No, they cannot be using the source." This is the radiation pill which comes out of a leaded box and radiates through to the film. But this was an x-ray machine which goes up the pipe and takes a picture on the film after developing.

We ran up to the truck and asked, "Is the source out?" The reply was, "Yes." "Check your dose meter," I said. We all had them. It tells how much radiation you have had in one day. It was off the screen. God knows how much we had taken in.

There was a huge argument because they should have put signs out to stop people from coming too close. They thought that being in the middle of nowhere, no one would come. Also, they were on a scam, which was rife over there. The Saudi contractors would pay you money in hand if you would spend all day on the same joint that would produce the work to finish sooner. But no one knew that the rest of the welding on the other joints was subpar. Later, I shall tell you how shit like that does not work.

The lads were telling us that they got Rolexes, money, booze, etc. It was a dodgy game if you were caught.

Gamma radiography at the time

Gamma radiography was introduced 40 years ago as a supplement to X-ray radiography to provide a means of inspecting and casting welded assemblies and any other engineering structures for internal defects such as blowholes and cracks. This method of non-destructive testing had been developed alongside X-ray inspection.

We said our goodbyes to the 2 lads and said we shall not mention you in dispatch. You owe us big time; this got me thinking there's good money to be made out here, but that was not to come for a few years yet.

Got back to camp and went to the superintendent, a Welsh cunt who did not like the English, and I had no time for the fucker either. Remember the Welsh cunt on the course he was in our camp right up the superintendent's arse up to his toenails, so we told him what had happened. We made a story up that did not sound convincing, but he took it, hook line and sinker. Told us to give him the blue radiation badges, and they would be sent to UK, hoping they would come back.

We had overdosed on radiation, and they would have to pay us up and send us home. However, that was not going to happen. Eight weeks down the line, we asked if they had any report from London and got a reply that it got lost in transit, which fucking stinks. We were given orders only to do minimal radiography and give it to someone else to do. Well, that was right up my street. I could never work out the development times when I was on the course and still did not know. I used to guess the time in the development room and still did, and it worked. Bullshit! Again working, so things were going smoothly now. I worked in the morning, swam for an hour at dinner time, and then worked for five more hours in the afternoon. After that, I had a drink as the sun went down. Not a bad life, I thought, but there are always some things that are going to bite you in the arse. I was driving back to camp where a local Saudi smashed into me not a good thing for an expat the police came I was arrested and put in a cell.

I was put into a cell with a Welsh man. I said to him, "How long have you been here?" He said, "5 months, fucking hell, bro. What did you do?" He then explained he went to a party with his mate, which is a no outside of camp. Got into his truck, and his mate had walked up the road. Rather than driving back, this fucker ran him over. He panicked and went back to the camp and left him. The next morning, they found him with 2 broken legs and a broken collarbone. That's when they got him to the hospital. They automatically take a booze test and are found positive. They then arrested him. He was in the hospital for a month, then discharged and put in isolation in his room till the court case, which could be 12 months' time. The police checked every truck on the compound and found some evidence on the Welsh man's car, so he was charged and is now in jail. When in jail, they did not feed you; the company feeds you.

After hearing all this, I was now shitting myself. I was charged and put in jail with no blanket or food and never slept a wink. The next morning, when my firm found out, I got some breakfast: cold egg on toast and a jug of orange juice. Around 10 pm, I was released. I found out that the Arab's father was the owner of all the Wimpy trucks, so he would not press charges. The police did say that I was 100 percent to blame, and if I were not in the country, this would not have happened. I got a bollocking and got picked up back to camp to the fucking Welsh tosser. He gave me a bollocking, saying, "You are costing this company money with all that's happening to you." So, I thought, "What a knob. I'd love to see you back in the UK on a one-to-one." At this time, you were allowed two leaves a year, so around three months, you could take your first leave. I put in a request and was told I could go in two weeks' time. So, I spent the time looking at what I could do once I returned back, which I would many times. I told you earlier about the lads stopping on one weld all day, knowing it was 100 percent right. This means the pipeline only needs 25 percent X-ray on the butts, meaning the pipeline will be finished quicker, and the Arab contracting firm would make plenty of money. I saw what can happen when this trick is played out.

One night, I was woken up, and the room was shaking from a very big explosion. The next day, we heard that the Gas Oil Separation Plant (GOSP) had blown up. In the first week, they blamed the Israelis. I had to go to this plant to do a small X-ray. When I arrived, there were two spheroids imploded, and the whole site was in pieces. There was a team of American investigators there, and they told me what they had found out. There was a rupture in one of the gas lines. These are 40 inches in diameter and welded, but they found slag inclusion on the weld, meaning it was never x-rayed. The gas went downstream, hit the flare line, caught fire, burnt all the way back to the pipe, into the pipe, then on the vessels, which imploded and then burnt all the plant. That taught me a big lesson. If you are going to do something like that, do the job, get paid by the contractor, and before it goes online, take the money and run. End of story.

Well, my time to go on vacation had arrived, and I knew I would not return for a while. I had a good woman back home who I wanted to marry, so I left one evening not to return for 6 years. But what 6 years that was! On a footnote, when I was out there, I bought a book from the camp shop called The Blue Flame. While it had no author or corporate logo, anyone who lived in K.S.A. and worked for Aramco until the late 1990s probably had one. Just because alcohol is not allowed in a Muslim country, at least we should do it safely. There were still rooms that got blown up with ex-pats letting them run dry, and then boom! Then they had to throw six to get out of jail LOL.

As I mentioned earlier about the Welsh man in jail, I got to know the lad he ran over. He was in our camp, and he did 12 months confined to the camp till it went to court. He was found guilty, as was the driver. Because they had done 12 months, they were deported back to the UK. They had no pay for a year. What a fucking company! I met him a couple of times back in the UK, but now I've lost touch.

Well, I arrived home with a radio, plenty of money, and plenty of cassettes, all country and western. I had them for many years, and all bought back memories.

Now was the time to court and bullshit Susan into marrying me, which we did. So my quest to make big money was still at the back of my mind. I lost my job the week after getting married. I got a job in Gee Cross the week I got back from my honeymoon. It lasted 3 days, and you had to use your own toilet paper. I told them to shove the job up their arses. But at that time, you could just walk from job to job. I went to work at Trafford Park for a while, contracting as a fitter on many sites. It was during this time that we decided to buy a shop. Bad move. We bought the shop; it was a general store mini-market that sold everything.

The first day in the shop, a posh lady came in and asked for a packet of STs. I thought they were cigarettes. I said, "We don't have those cigarettes." She said, "No, sanitary towels." I said, "Oh," walked down to the bottom of the shop, and shouted while the shop was full, "Do you want Tampax, Super Lilets, Doctor White, or Extra?" She whispered, "Tampax Super." I got a box, put it on the counter, and said, "1.50." She then said, "Can you wrap it up?" I never saw her again. It was going great guns for the first year, then I opened up next door as a greengrocer's shop and wet fish, and I had a game license. This was when things started to slide down. I made a gibbet to hang my rabbits on, just like they did in Victorian times, and on the wall, I put up a blackboard that said, "You have read the book and seen the film, now eat the stars." On the first day, children and mothers going up to school started crying. There was a public outcry in the village. I had to take them down, so I put on the board, "Freshly shot rabbits daily." That was a total lie. I used to go once a month, shoot a load, take them back to the shop, gut them, put them in bags, and freeze them.

Well, this one day, an old woman came in, called Mrs. Smith. She said, "I have not had a fresh rabbit since the war. Could you go out and shoot me one tomorrow?" I said, "Of course." When she left, I got one out of the freezer.

The next day, I re-bagged it and gave it to Mrs. Smith. One hour later, she came back and said, "Mr. Oldham, how many rabbits did you shoot this morning?" I said, "Just the one." "Well, can you tell me why it's got 4 back legs?" she asked. I never saw her again. What happened was when I was cleaning the rabbits and cutting them up, I accidentally put four back legs into one bag. Someone else must have had the bag with 4 front feet in it, but they never came back.

By this time, I was well-known in the village as a rebel. There was a day in the village when the gypsies came. They started at the top shops. The women came in with hordes of kids and started pinching what they could. I was told about this, so I got one of the shotguns and put it on the counter. When they came to my shop, they saw the shotgun through the window and bypassed my shop. They then went to the post office to cause havoc. That got around the village and surrounding areas that this man must not be messed about with. I did not find that out for many years after.

Then one day, one of my dogs died in the shop in front of the counter. I was out at the time. Susan said to the customer, "He was asleep." The dog was dead with a turd sticking out of its arse. At this time, I was shooting mad. I used to go up to Scotland with my mate shooting geese while Susan was looking after the shop. Looking back now, I was and still am a chauvinistic cunt.

One day, I arrived home with a goose. I said, "I am having it stuffed," which I did. I went to collect it, and I forgot I wanted its wings open to look like it was landing. Well, it must have been 5 foot wide. I got back to the shop, and I couldn't get it through the shop door. Susan said, "You are not bringing that fucker in here!" So I gave it away. Really, it was too big of a thing, alright for a stately home lol.

Now, I was hitting the drink every night in the pub as the business was slowly going down the tubes. I came up with a cunning plan. I had an outhouse at the back of the shop that used to have grocers in it, but all it held was cardboard. I decided to set fire to it and claim on the insurance. I waited for a day when my mother and father were here. I lit the cardboard, then called my dad and said, "We're on fire!" We could not slack the fire out, and the next door had a greenhouse full of hens - or should I say 12 plus. As the flames went higher, their bedroom window was open, and their curtains were being sucked out of the window, ready to catch fire. We phoned the fire brigade, and they came with 2 fire engines trapping us in the shop with all the village kids robbing me of my sweets. A fireman asked my mother have you any more children? My mother replied not bloody likely one is enough he will be the death of me. They got the fire out, but unfortunately, I killed all the hens and had to pay for them. Additionally, I was not insured as it had run out.

We tried to sell the shop, but only an Asian wanted it for half price. We sold it to him and went to Germany to work so I could get a mortgage. We left the shop with 40 pounds to our name, but we bought a townhouse back in the village, and you guessed it, the talk was "I knew he would not make it." We were in debt to some tune and were paying off small amounts monthly. It came to a point where I got a letter to go to the queen's bench for debt I owed. I was working in Germany at the time, but Susan sorted it out with tears. She went to court with my Farther to be told when I came back to the country I would be arrested she was told it was a formality and she did not take it lightly.

This was a roller-coaster ride, and we could not get any lower. When I came back from Germany, I worked nights putting tops on fairy liquid bottles for 12 hours a night, but I knew in my heart that someday something would go right for us.

Then I saw an ad in the paper for work in Saudi for a job at Jeddah airport as a Foreman working with TCNs (third-class nationals). I applied, told them I could do this and that, and I got the job. Also with the help of my mother in law who looked after the children. Susan went to work in children's nursery through the day and then did a evening shift at a old folks home to get us back on track.

It is better to be someone in your own village than no one in a metropolis.

The day arrived to start my new job. I never had Sue come to the airport. I just played "Leaving on a Jet Plane" and caught a taxi to the airport. I knew I had to get my shit together. I never had pictures of my children or Susan, for that matter. I had seen grown men cry for their children and wives out there. It's a shit hole of a place, and I do think its any better now. They still stone women, but they now do it the humane way. They dig a hole, put the woman in a sack, tie it up, put the woman in the hole, and a lorry tipped big rocks on her. Fucking barbaric. Then they cut your hand off for stealing, and it's always the right hand. The left hand is for wiping your arse, so it's a double whammy. You cannot sit down at a table with someone to eat, as they have to feed you. You cannot use your left hand.

So I landed in Jeddah and got picked up and taken to the camp, middle of nowhere as it happens. Got my key and found my room, not a thing in it, only a desk, a bed, and a chair. That was it for 4 months. Fuckin' hell. But in years to come, I got used to that turning up to a bed and a chair, but one day I knew I would be on a winner.

Had breakfast, met some of the guys from the airport and met my boss, who I got on with. He had another Foreman who was okay but full of himself. I always become the grey man when I first get on a new job.

I didn't talk much. I find the less you talk, the more they think you know what you are talking about. You can open your mouth and drop yourself in it. The boss drove me to the airport facility where our workshops were; the tradesmen were Bangladeshi. They were a happy lot, but I did have a run-in with them later on. We had turners, fitters, sheet metal workers, welders, plus some semi-skilled workers.

On the first day, we drove around the outer perimeter of the airport, which was very large indeed. It was split into 5 terminals north and south terminal, the Royal terminal, and the Hajj terminal. This was only open when it was Hajj, and there was the Royal hanger which housed all the kings and wife's planes, but we shall come back to this king's hanger later. After being shown around the airport and being told our role at the airport, I thought, piece a piss now the boss told me he was leaving and someone had to take his place, not the other forman but me. Let's go for it. This job at the airport was a good grounding for me later and taught me how to manage people and not make them think they are worth less.

So, let's begin the 2nd day. I had a driving test and got all my permits etc. the next thing was to be taught how to drive on the airside, day and night; there were strict rules if you went in front of a plane taxing, it could be half a mile away, but you go to jail. I took the day test, and I passed, but the night one was very scary. All the different runways had different colored lights past that, but I would not be driving at night fuck that.

Our job was to maintain the airport at all times. We had 3 shirts and ties to wear when going into the terminals and had work ware for site work. The first week was getting used to everything and finding the camp when finished. It was around 15 miles away in the shit hole of Jeddah. We were next to a scrap yard. There was an old guy who was in his late fifties. I got to know him. He had just gotten divorced, and he needed the money. This was the time I got onto Jedder gin. My boss was a past master at it. I was going to get all the gear myself and start brewing. All you needed was yeast, sugar and fruit with water in that heat. It was drinkable in 2 weeks, 5 gallons of gin, and that should last you till the next batch. Oh, you needed bottles, so you bought and stole them. They were grape juice bottles with a spring-loaded top.

Had many good nights on the old Jeddah gin. Well, I was working up to get the supervisor's job doing okay and not rocking the boat much, then I got an e-mail that I had the job and the other foreman was leaving as well, so this will leave me shorthanded but fuck it. I thought going up the ranks now and for sure it was an upward climb over the years. I did make it, as you will see later in the book. Well, the day came when the two left, and now I was on my own with 20 Bangladeshis.

The first day no problem, then the biggest Bangy of the group came up to me demanding this and that, so I waited till he had finished. I fucked him up and down dale, which was a wrong move. The first mistake, he got the rest of the guys to do very little work, and they kept asking me how do you do this and that for things they knew. They had me by the balls. I had to get the work done that I used to get in from other departments, but these fuckers were having none of it. This big fucker needs to be taken down as I had 3 weeks of this shit. There was a great flood in Bangladesh people had been washed away, a real to-do out there, so these lads wanted to go home to see if their parents were dead etc. etc. at the time, there was no e-mail etc. It was by writing.

I let a couple go on leave when this big cunt for a Bangladeshi came into my office and said he would like to take his leave home early to sort his house out what was flooded or washed away. I said no, he then broke down in tears. I said to him "You had made my life shite, but I tell you what you tell your lads, I am the big boss, and not you. I will let you go home", which he did, and 2 days later, he went home, never to return. I stopped that fucker from coming back, so it was back on the Jeddah Gin and happy times, or so I thought. A week passed no problem getting all the hours in the job, which was good.

Another episode happened one Friday when I was off and was just going for dinner. I mentioned I would hope the sun bleaches my hair before going home. Nothing like blond hair for the ladies. This old guy said, "When I was younger, we used to put butter on our hair to turn it blond" as he said it. My eye saw on the table packets of butter, little single packs. I took the lot and went back to my room. Had a few drinks, which was a wrong move, then I put this butter on my hair, went down to the pool and went to sleep. When I woke up, there must have been a million flies on my head and face where this butter had melted. I did not know what the fuck was going on. I jumped into the pool; there was a fucking great oil slick on top of the water. I never did that again.

The next incident happened when I got a call to go to the Royal hanger, so I drove round to the hanger. This is where the king had his planes which are many. It's a great big hanger when I arrived there were 4 planes in the hanger. The main king's plane was out, and thank fuck for that. The security was tight, but I had all the passes. I went to the superintendent, who was a Brit. He took me outside to show me on the roof that a security camera had toppled over the roof, and I was to replace the bracket for the camera.

I logged it all down, looked at the job and thought fuck me, I am not climbing up there to look at it, so I returned to base, got work permits, fire permits etc., sorted, then I took 4 men and a mobile welding set with a new bracket. This took hours to get things sorted, so I showed the lads the job and, as they always said, "No problem, Mr. Peter". So, I left them to it. I then drove around the airport to see how the rest of the teams were doing.

It was around 3 hours later that I got a call on the radio to make haste to the royal terminal. When I arrived, the guys were outside screaming and shouting at me "oh, Mr. Peter kalabush" meaning prison. I said just one of you talk he said just come with me he opened the door, low and behold, all I could see was fucking foam. He said 3 planes are surrounded by foam.

Oh fuck, I thought this was it. Me and lads are in jail, never to be released. The kings planes were covered in foam. I had to sort this shit out at the side of the hangar people were panicking they thought they would go to jail. I got them all to listen to me first. Let's find out what started the foam cannons which were placed all inside the hanger. I found out that plane tyers can ignite 30 minutes after touch down; by that time, the planes would be in the hangar out of preying eyes unless they went to the royal terminal, which I will mention later.

I had a good idea of what happened, so I went step by step with my men, and what they did was they took the old bracket off, put the new bracket on the roof and started to weld, but they struck up on the thin roof which sent sparks down below and this set of the fire foam guns the foam was up to the doors. Now I got all my work permits out and checked to see if this was the right day to start. Found out it was so we were in the clear of the superintendent's maintenance crew, did not have to lock them off. I found out he went to jail for god knows how long. That's how it was then, and I bet it still is. The superintendent put his notice in and fucked off before they could pin something on him a lucky day for us. Back to base for a stiff cup of tea off the lads and a stiff drink at night to tell my tale to the rest of the lads on site.

The next drop bollock was when I was having a drive around the airport, tossing it off just listening to Dire Straits with my arm out of the window, thinking of a summer's day in the UK. When I came to a security hut with a barrier across the road. I stopped to go through when I saw 2 of the lads doing planned maintenance on the motor and gears of the barrier. I drove round to the side and went into the cabin.

There were 2 guys, one Saudi guard and one Pilipino guard. I started to talk to one of the guards when my periphery vision saw a sign-up, and down while talking, I pressed the up sign of one of the buttons and thought nothing of it till one of the guys came in from airside and said, "Mr. Peter" gash on the floor no more went round and sure enough the fuckers on the floor and his eyes back of his head all I could see was wright of his eyes. I said, "What the fuck happened," the other guy said, "Gears go round, fingers go in" He looked at his finger, and sure enough, 2 fingers were squashed. How did it happen by just operating the button? Now I am in deep shit. I took him to the hospital then they transferred him to a third-rate hospital because that's what his firm paid for; I got back to base and made a report that went straight to management. I said while in the cabin, someone must have pressed the button, and the barrier went down, and that's how he got trapped with his fingers plus, I did put down that they should have isolated the machine before working on it.

3 hrs. later, the Filipino, who was in the cabin, got pulled over the coals. So, they had their own mafia and their top lad came to see me and said don't blame my lad for what you did, or there will be consequences for you. So, I made an attachment to my first letter stating that 100 percent blame should go to the maintenance team for

not isolating the equipment. This was accepted, and it went to be filed 3 days later. The lad was on sick leave. I went to his room to see him; he was not happy. He knew I pressed the button, plus they did not chop the tops of his fingers off.

They just bandaged them up and said they would heal. I knew they were fucked. They looked like flippers on his hand, plus he was on half-pay. Then the rest of the team started to badger me to pay the rest of his pay because it was me who pressed the button. I found out that the philopena mafia had put the word out; it was not one of these men but me. By this time, I was getting some flak from the lads again, asking how do you do this and that so making my life harder. This was now the time to go on leave and look for other things abroad, but this was a great learning curve on how to treat men and how to get the best out of them.

I remember I had to spend a Christmas there, and this was the first Christmas of many on my life's journey. I had to work. I remember going to the terminal where the last flight went to get back to the UK for Christmas and saw them all waiting there, laughing and joking. Then they went on the plane. I can say there was a tear in my eye having to stop in this shit hole of a country.

This brings me back to the chopping of heads, hands and stoning women. The majority of death sentences are carried out in public by beheading, drawing comparisons with the shocking brutality of the Islamic state, which Britain will come to in 3 generations. The system is based on Shariah law, which the Saudis say is rooted in Islamic tradition and the Quran trials are reported to have lasted a day and confessions extracted under torture. The country has no written penal code and no code of criminal procedure and judicial procedure. That allows courts wide power to determine what constitutes a criminal offence and what sentences the crimes deserve. The only means of appeal is directly to the king, who decides whether the condemned lives or dies.

The list of punishments makes for grim reading. One of the cases was five Yemenis were beheaded, then their heads were re-attached and then left hanging for all to see. Floggings are on a daily basis.

In the first 4 months of 2018 alone, 86 beheadings were carried out. Beheading remains the most common form of execution, and the sentence is traditionally carried out in a public square on Friday prayers. Plus, the Mutawa religious police used to find contractors and make them watch the beheadings. I can say I did not get picked at any stage being out there. Deera Square in the center of Riyadh is known as chop square in Saudi the practice of crucifixion refers to the court-ordered public display of the body after execution, along with the separated head if beheaded.

Stoning remains a punishment for adultery for women in Saudi. The accused are put into holes and then have rocks tipped on them from a truck. There has not been a stoning for years. This is the humane way of doing it now.

Eye gouging can be given to you for fighting with a Saudi.

Amputation of limbs is another of the horrific punishments in the country, and it's your right hand because you wipe your arse with your left.

Flogging those convicted of insulting Islam can also expect to be flogged with up to 1000 lashes.

High-way robbery is punished by cross amputation, which involves the removal of the right hand and left foot.

I knew this was not the job I was really wanting. The money was good but not the best, I was thinking again, which is not always the right way to go sometimes, I spent Christmas there and got pissed most nights but did find out after Christmas day that Christmas was as far away as it can be, and that helped me down the line of how to spend and think about Christmas. It's no good having pictures of your family on your desk and walls at times like that. You only get sad and want to be home, another lesson in life's great tapestry.

We used to have small cars to go about the airport. There was one incident that amused me, but not for the 2 men in the car. They got behind a jumbo jet when it fired up its engine's for testing. When it turned the engines on to full power, it blew the car like tumbleweed down the runway and rolled it over and over. When the security and fire brigade got there, they were still alive, and all their main clothing had been blown off. They went with the police to spend time in jail. That's how it was then, and I bet it still is.

On the other side of the airport, it was the RASAVE Saudi royal air force. There was an incident over there when 2 Indian cleaners were gang raped and put in hospital by their air force personnel.

We heard weeks later no one was charged. They were just TCNs third-class nationals lower than a snake's belly.

Some of the lads, when in town on a Friday, were taken by the religious police to chop square to witness a beheading; they were told this is what happens if you break the law. The square would be clear to make way for the execution to take place. After the beheading of the condemned, the head is stitched to the body, which is wrapped up and taken away for final rites. You can see what state the guys were in when they got back on camp.

There were many funny-looking Saudis. This was due to interbreeding. We talked to 2 British midwives who said there were many babies born disfigured as fuck and riddled with diseases, because of interbreeding.

Well, it was time for me to go from this shit hole for a time, but I wanted to go on the West Coast again. That was where the money was. I would have to bullshit for a job out there, but I was getting good at that. Plus, I found out that the people who were in charge of you were not as good as you thought they were.

Once you have bullshitted your way out there, they are not going to send you home because it costs them too much. They will slot you into something but the pay is still the same; get my drift you are only out there for the money, not like a few people I have seen who get a woman, and before you know it, they are spending money on them and sending fuck all to a wife back home.

Bad move there were incidents where the wife found out. When they had gone back on leave, their house gone, dog gone, wife gone, no money in the bank. In Jeddah, I used to sell my blood every 2 weeks to pay for presents for when I was on leave; it's all about saving money for your retirement. Well, I flew out of Jeddah on Wednesday evening. There was not a tear in my eye. I knew I could do better, but this would not be for a few years yet as I had to learn a few more skills.

DON'T LET YESTERDAY TAKE UP TOO MUCH OF TODAY

After returning home, I had to find a job. I was talking to a guy who was looking for men to work in London for 2 years, coming home most weekends. It was at the P.O. building, which was having a revamp, and we were the pipe fitters on the job. I had done a little pipe fitting, but not on this scale, but it would be another belt in my armoury for when the big job comes off, and I knew it would happen, though how long I did not know. The first job when we got to London was to find some digs. We found it in Finsbury Park, a hotel across the road from the park. We found out later that it was once owned by the Krays.

We got settled in and went on site. I looked at what we had to do, and I knew it was a ball acre of a job. I was there for 18 months, I got myself into a few scrapes in the bar at night, but nothing to get bothered about. The lads who I went with were all younger than me, bar another guy we called Yak, and they all liked a joint or two. You can imagine what states we got into and the places we went for breakfast. We plodded on with the job, but after 12 months, I got itchy feet, and the money was crap.

I started to look for jobs back in the Middle East. I found one straight away, applied, and got an interview in Dubai. It was a job I did not want, but I could have a night in Dubai and fly back home all in a weekend. I thought a little break was costing me now, so I told my boss what I was doing and said "Good luck, but when I said I did not want the job, he looked at me strangely."

So, on a Thursday morning, I flew into Dubai at night, got to the hotel around 11 pm, had a couple of drinks, woke up and had breakfast, ate everything I could. I got picked up to go for an interview, filled in a few forms, had a one-to-one. I completed it in one hour and thought this is it, finished and back to the hotel on the lash then back home at night. Not so, there was a 2-hour written test, so I did it in one hour, told them I was going, and could not have a second interview to see if I had passed, which I knew I had not. I said, "Email me my results today later on."

So, I got a lift back to the hotel and down to the bar, had a great time, went back to my room to pack my gear, and get to the airport and jet back home. While I was out, the company was phoning me and sent somebody to collect me back to the office. I was having none of that. I got to the airport, flew out, and went back to work on Monday. What a gem, I thought; I got expenses of the company, many phone calls which I never answered. Back in the real world now.

I made no big deal of it, but the lads at the bar Monday night were gobsmacked. To me, it was life's great tapestries - get back on track, which I did. Then, I saw an ad for a mechanical superintendent for a French firm. I found out later they wanted someone else on their team. They had just sacked someone doing this job, and it was getting near Christmas, so they wanted someone badly. I put in for the job, got a phone interview, lied that I could speak a little French, and bullshitted about the job. In 24 hrs, I had gotten the job. It was in Abu Dhabi for 4 weeks, then on-site, which was on an island called Zerku, to commissioning this plant that was going to be put online. I thought I would learn some shit on this job, so I accepted it, and bingo! I was flying out for a week. My wife, by this time, was not really upset. This was becoming the norm, but time would tell on this job. I took on more than I could chew.

I flew out to Abu Dhabi on Monday morning. I never had Susan come to the airport. Two reasons, one, I had to get my shit together before flying, and two, I'm a bit of a softy, really. But this time, she did come, and I got a bit homesick, to say the least when I left her to go airside. This was not like me, so I had an inclination this was going to be a bit of a rough trip. Plus, I was going out as a commission engineer - never was and never will be - but I was going for the drive. I thought I could learn on the job, not to be.

I arrived at around 11 pm. That was the time most UK flights arrived in the Middle East. I went through customs, which took around 2 hours - the norm. Then I got picked up and went to my digs, which were in the same building as the office. Before flying out to Zercu, I woke up early to a telephone call from the agent who got me the job with this French oil company. He gave me the details of the office and phone number if I needed them, and they would send someone round with my ID, and they would take my passport off me, which was the norm.

I did remember that I only had one page left in my passport. This was going to be a lifeline in the next few months. They came for my passport as I was having breakfast. I gave them the passport, and they then took me down to an office where I would be working and meeting the guys who I would be with. I was introduced to the boss, who spoke to me in French. He must have thought I could speak French. I was introduced to the commissioning electrician (French), the hydraulics engineer (French), and the bloody vibration and instrument engineer - all French. I was shown my table and filing cabinet.

I was next to the electrician. He did speak English but was not good at coming forward. This was the time computers were just coming online in the offices. All the French had their own, and I had nothing.

It really started on the first day. I found out the man I was taking over from was French, and this project had been going on for 3 months. They were already nearly ready to go onto the island. They were waiting for me to get my shit together about the job and how I was going to implement the mech commissioning of the project.

I started to find out what the last man had done, but he had thrown away everything he had done. Now, this was a bummer. I really did not know where to start. In another office, I had an Indian who would do all my typing as I was doing it longhand.

The first day was tough, and no one came to me to see how I went on or if I needed anything. I was left to my own devices. So, I went back to my room and went to the restaurant, hoping to see some of the lads. Well, it was a bit of a disappointment. There were plastic tablecloths, and you helped yourself to the food they put out. Plus, the lads who were on my project had other accommodations outside of the building.

I finished my tea and went back to my room, thinking of what the fuck am I supposed to do. I did not know how to start a report, let alone do it long-hand. Then I had a brainwave. I shall go back to the office and rummage around the other lads' work to find a starting point of how to make some type of document which would at least bullshit them.

I went back to the office, had a word with security that I was working late, and went through the startup procedure of the electrician and the instrument engineers' documents. I wrote down how they formatted it and took bullet points. I now had a base on how to start my startup document. This was the time before Google; it would have been easy now. So, I put everything back as it was and went back to my room, jotting things down for tomorrow.

The next day arrived, and I came into the office saying good morning to the boring bastards. No reply, only grunts. Oh well, fuck me, I thought. Well, I started writing my startup procedure, and I made myself aware of the scribe who was going to make it into a document. I put some money in his hand to really help me out with the task involved.

Now, after the second night in, I thought I must find a place for a drink to pass the time of day. It was the Nova Hotel, which was around a 15-minute walk away. We used to get around 20 pounds a day to buy things for dinner and tea. So, what I did was I used to go to the bar and buy a pint and ask for nuts and popcorn. That was my tea.

I could afford 6 pints a day, which was not bad through the week, but at weekends, we were not working so, I had to do other things like walking from one end to the other on the seafront. The French lads never asked me round to their place. If truth be known, I was doing a better job than they thought I could do, but this was with the help of my scribe and his friends, who were mech engineers. After around 4 weeks and still no pay, I was told to get my shit together. We are going to move to Zerku Island to finish the job, and you will commission the Mechanical side of things.

"Oh shit," I thought. "Remember, this is a multi-million-pound project, and I am the lead guy to commission it on the mech side of things. This was when I started to panic." We went to the airport with the French altogether, and I was in a taxi to the private airport to catch a plane to the island. It was an hour flying, and I thought, "Well, I am bollocks now once I get over there." We flew out with no problems, got to my digs which were very nice, and we went for a nice lunch. In the afternoon, we went on-site, where I was taken to this Brit who had built this gas oil separation plant, i.e., GOSP. He was telling me what we had to do, or I had to check with calculations, the feed of oil, etc. By this time, I was in over my head. I had run, not walked, up to this position, but unknown to me, this was a great learning point for years to come. However, it did not look that way at the time. The first night,

I got no sleep thinking about how the fuck am I going to get out of this. The next day, I got an office and all the paperwork I had to sign when I had commissioned every part of the plant. Knowing what I know now, I should not have panicked because I have found out that all jobs get finished with or without you, and there is always someone who will help you. But this did not register with me.

All I wanted to do was get the fuck out of dodge; how I did not know. I tried to phone Sue and ask her to tell them that my mum was dead. She would not do it. I kept phoning Susan, panicking, the first time ever that I was over my depth. Then, at tea one night, I was speaking to a Brit who put bums on seats at the airport to fly back to the mainland. I told him my tale, and he said, "Be at the airport at 5 am tomorrow. I will get you on the first plane out, and then you are on your own." Sure enough, the next morning, I turned up with a little bag (I forgot my leather coat. I hope someone made good use of it), boarded the plane, and fucked off from Zerku, never to return.

But now I had to plan what's next. Remember, I had no passport; my agent had it. So when I landed, I got a taxi to the office, went in, and introduced myself. I started to bullshit, telling them they wanted me to stay on the island longer than my contract said, and this would be having to work through Christmas. So they sent me over to the mainland for a couple of days' rest before flying out again. Then I said, while I am here, I will take my passport and take it to the embassy for a few more pages to be put in my passport. As I said earlier, I knew that I had only one page left. He went to the safe, got my passport, and checked to see if I was correct. He then gave it to me and said I had to bring it back to him in 2 days.

Now I was on a roll. I then asked, "Can I have a sub for the booze and hotel I will be stopping in?" He took me to the cashier, who gave me £500. I signed for it and said, "See you in a couple of days." I went to a travel agent for a ticket to London. I got one for the same night. I spent the afternoon in a hotel bar, just hoping no one knew me, but in hindsight, no one gave a fuck. That night, I got a plane to London, then one to Manchester, and finally, I was home to my beloved with my tail between my legs.

It was a couple of days later when the company from England phoned me and asked, "What the fuck are you doing at home?" I told him I had not gotten paid, the job was shit, and I escaped out of Zerku, got my passport, and fucked off back home. And if I don't get all my money this week, I am going to the press. He did say that I would be blacklisted from ever going back to the Middle East. I said, "Give it your best shot."

Four days later, I got what I was owed and still had the £500. Happy days.

Sometimes you have to let yourself break down before you can build yourself up.

I returned to the UK feeling defeated and regrouped. I was a man with his tail between his legs. I needed to learn more about the oil fields, so I got a job with a company that worked offshore. They were now starting onshore at the power stations around the UK during the shutdowns that occurred in the spring. The company was called Grey Tool UK, but it is now bankrupt. However, I didn't think it was all because of me. I was hired as an in situ engineer, which meant I worked on-site machining parts that couldn't be taken off to be taken to the workshop. This job was right up my street since I served my time as a centre lathe turner.

I started on a windy, wet morning in Manchester. I remember looking at the workshop, which was in Disarray, meaning they were winging it. I got to know the entire team during the first week and met the lad who I would be teamed up with. We would be spending days away on site. After the first week in the workshop, we were sent to a power station near Lincoln to suss out the job and make a tool to turn these flanges.

We set off, and this lad was a bit strange, to say the least. We got along well. We got to the site and spent all day on a safety briefing. Additionally, we had to spend the first night in a pub. We got to the digs and went for a pint, which continued all night. Our dinner was in the pub, and after around three hours of drinking, this lad, let's call him Tom, went for a piss. When he came back, he said, "There's a great picture in the bog, and said that's mine." Never thinking anything about it, I said nothing, and we continued drinking. I went to bed, and he followed later.

The next morning we went for breakfast, paid the bill, and went on-site. When I opened the back of the van, what was there? The fucking picture. I said, "What the fucking hell did you do?" He just smiled and said, "Get in," and we fucked off to the site. We then got on the site, took measurements, and went back to the workshop to spend a week modifying a machine that would do the job. We returned a week later to spend a week there. I was dreading what this fucker would be getting up to on-site, as we were told not to use machinery that belonged to the power station, which would bite us in the arse later on.

The first night we spent in a hotel, the same thing happened - he started pinching soap, towels, and anything he could put his hands on. That was the first night. We booked out of that hotel the next day, saying to me it was a little expensive. After that, we booked into this lovely old-fashioned pub with a beautiful garden at the back. The next morning, he said we needed to arrive on site early. So, we paid the bill and went on our merry way. On the way to the site, he said, "Wait till you open the back." We got to site and opened the back door - it was full to the brim with all the shrubs from the garden. I said, "Fuck me, if we get caught with this lot, we will go to jail." He then said, "Stop moaning." That was it - I got him by the throat and said, "Don't mess with me." After that, we never spoke again.

That day, we went back to base and told the supervisor that I was leaving. He already knew what this tosser was like, but he was on the books, and I was just a contractor. So, I told them to stick to their job. He asked me if I would work the week out with someone else at Fiddler's Ferry, and I said yes. So off we went with another permanent staff. He said the other bloke was a pain offshore, and he was the same. When we got to Fiddler's Ferry, we went through safety procedures, etc.

Same thing, don't use any equipment that belongs to the site. The job was to trepan four holes in the lady legs, which are 30-inch pipes that attach to the turbine to bring steam to turn them. Our job was to cut four round holes and save the disk to show the safety department that we did not drop them into the turbine.

What happened was the first hole, the magnet which would hold the disk, was not on, and when we punched through, the disk dropped down into the turbine. This was deep shit time. It would take weeks to strip this thing down and retrieve the disk. We were panicking at this time. I said, "Let's do the rest. I will go to a couple of contractors to see if they can burn us a disk, and I will clean the sides up." The other lad machined out the disks, and I had a disk manufactured and cleaned up just like the rest of them. We then took them to the safety officer, who booked down all disks present and correct. We would be long gone when they fire the turbine up. Plus, in my mind, they should be a strainer there anyhow to catch all the crap which can be forced down with the steam. Anyhow, we were on a roll. We started to take the gear down to the van, which was four floors. I said, "Fuck this; let's put them in the lift, and it will only take one trip." Well, we loaded up the lift and went down. The doors opened, and fuck me, a safety man and a security team were there. We were screwed. We had used their equipment. We were thrown off-site after a fucking bollocking. I was a bit wild in those days. I knew I was leaving this company anyhow, so I told them in no uncertain words to shove their job and site where the sun doesn't shine. We were then escorted right out of the gates, never to return. Well, you can imagine what was said back at the base.

How we lost them 6 months of work, and once again, I told them to shove it. Six months later, that firm went bankrupt. I wonder why.

I went on the shutdowns then, all around Trafford Park and beyond. It was during this time I saw a job for mechanical technicians, and one of them was mechanical back in Saudi on the west coast. That was where the money was.

I got an interview in London and was told I was going to do three years up in Tanajib. Tanajib takes oil from the Mjan oil field and is located on the eastern coast of the Arabian Gulf, also known as the Persian Gulf. It is and still is operated by Saudi Arabia's state-owned oil and gas company, Saudi Aramco. It has an offshore field as well. The daily crude oil now is around 300,000 barrels a day.

At the interview, I bullshitted, of course. It was around March 1991, just after Gulf War One had finished. I got the job. There were going to be three mechanical guys working on behalf of Aramco, watching and helping out the contractors on site. The main one was an American company called Fluor Daniel. The Fluor side of the company were from down south Texas and surrounding states. The Daniel side of it was from North America, New York, etc. They did not get on with each other.

So, I left my dear Susan once again at home to arrive at Manchester airport to catch a plane to Amsterdam, then a connecting flight to Saudi. I was on that plane flying to Amsterdam, shitting myself thinking, "What the fuck have I got myself into now?" I reached Amsterdam with no issues and went straight to the bar. This is where all expats meet before flying off to Middle Eastern countries. There, I met 2 guys on their second pint who came from up and around Newcastle. We hit it off from the start. One of the guys I got really pally with was Brenden Sperrin, a great lad who sadly died around 1999 of liver cancer. The grace of God go I.

We got on the plane half-pissed, knowing we were going to be out there for 4 months before coming home for RR. We arrived at

Dammam airport and waited to get through customs for 3 hours. It was always a pain in the arse to get through. We all got through and were picked up at arrivals by an Indian who took us to a compound for our first night. We got up first thing and waited until someone came to pick us up. The bungalow we were in had no food, just water, so we were hungry after our journeys. There was a knock on the door, and it was the driver to take us to the office to get processed. We arrived at the office to meet the boss of this company called, Marwarid. He was a Brit, a bit of a big head, telling us how he was here when the Scuds came in and how they all sat on the roofs watching the Scuds being shot down by the Patriots the Yanks had.

We were all jealous we were not there then, but in years to come, I would be in a war zone did not know that then though. We had the crack. We went for our security passes they took our passports off us. We had to wait a week to get everything, so we tossed it off by the pool and had a walk in the town at around 5 pm when it got cooler, it was over 100 degrees then.

So, the time came to pick up and drive to Tanajib, which takes about 4 hrs. I was shitting myself which was the norm I bullshitted getting the job so I did not know what to expect, Brenden on the other hand said I will be the pump man that was my job back in UK so I thought that's good new fuck all about pumps but I sure would by the end of three years, we arrived at Tanajib and met our superintendents Brendon got the pumps I got gas compressors and the other lad who I forgot his name got all the fans that cooled the pumps compressors etc., we found out that the plant had been moth balled around 6 years ago. The main contractor Fluro Daniel who we were going to supervise their work on the plant had made a gated compound a year earlier for all workers on site i.e. ex pats it was a large compound. We were shown the site and where we would be working. I went off with my superintendent to his office, and showed me what and where we shall start. I thought fucking hell, some fucking job. My job was to strip down 8 gas compressors to the ground, lift them off the bases get civils to do the concrete replace the base plates level them up and start to rebuild the compressors. My job title was senior mechanical technician. After a year it was upgraded to rotating and commissioning engineer.

The job in question was that I was seconded to Aramco for the installation of 8 Aces BFD2 stage pumps with 13.8Kv motors and the associated lube oil systems. Pre- and final commissioning of the equipment, including piping final alignment, carried out whilst supervising a multinational workforce, thus increasing Northern area pumping capacity. This would upgrade the crude oil to 60,000,000 bpd.

We were taken back to the camp and were told that we were the last people to arrive, so there will be a meeting in the main hall by the head of Fluor Darnels. We were wondering what the meeting was about, speculating about what it was. It was a great surprise when we all turned up, and it started: "All the people who like a drink stay, the people who don't can leave." You can imagine what we did. Yes, we stopped. The buildings on site were still being built; it was like a small town being built. The boss counted how many people liked a drink, remembering there is no drink in Saudi - more drunks than England though. He counted around 100, so he said: "Follow me." He took us to row upon row of houses, or should I say flats, which were back to back with a toilet and shower in the middle. You shared with the other person. He then said, "In the middle of the street, we are going to make a bar, and I need 3 people to run it." My hand went up, Brenden's hand went up, and my boss's hand went up. "Right, we have these three to run and make beer, wine, sadiqi, and run it like a business in their spare time. Big times ahead, me thinks."

So, the big boss brought bottles of whiskey to celebrate the new street we were going to have built with a bar in the middle. While the street was being built, the three of us got together and put a list together of what we needed to start the brewing process. We had to buy things singly and at different times so the Saudis did not get suspicious. We had a lock-up to put our brewing gear in. This was for the manufacture of wine, beer, and Jeddah gin. We found a source for the sadiqi. This is one of the first things you come across when you come to live in Saudi. Sid is short for Siddiqi, which means "my friend." Sid is a locally distilled spirit. A 5-gallon of uncut was around 50 pounds then, but you cut it with water 3 to 1, and it was still 70 percent and would wipe you out.

Most compounds populated by Westerners have access to mainly homemade wine and beer. Some of the compounds down in the cities even had competitions. The big thing with brewing was never to sell it, but we were running a bar and charging people to use it. Booze is a big thing on all compounds. They really are like little holiday camps. Some compounds smuggled in proper booze. We had to buy the Sid down in Al Kobar. Transporting alcohol around is fraught with danger due to the many roadblocks. The general rule is, so long as you kept it quiet on your compound, the police wouldn't bother you. But there were raids. We should be okay; we were in the middle of nowhere, and we bribed the guards on the gate to come and tell us if the police, or worst still, the religious police, were coming. They would come in and take everything, as well as you. If you got caught, there is only one to blame, and it's you.

Now, the Sid we were going to buy was a 4-hour journey one way and 4 hours back. That shitted me up, being caught before we got back to the job. The big boss gave us a phone number and an address down in Khobar to go and get the stuff. We were told to book into this compound; there were 3 bars in this compound. You would go down on a Friday night, book in the compound, and then phone up the number. You would go to his house to meet him, and he would tell you the ground rules. So it was started. When off the ground the trip would be every three weeks. We would go down to pick up 5 gals of Sid; this would make 15 gals. Another thing we did was send for Jack Daniels chips from America. There were barrels of Jack Daniels, which got cut up into small pieces. They were then put into a bottle of Sid, and the Jack Daniels wood chips would leach out and turn the Sid brown and give it a taste of Jack.

We got most of the stuff from the supermarket, but we needed sugar and wine juice, plus cases of near beer to turn it back to alcohol. So, we decided to take one of the trucks to Dammam, go to the compound, get the Sid, and then go to the supermarket for other brewing goods. I said, "That's a stupid thing to do, leaving five gallons of Sid in the truck. Let's get the Sid last." We made it down to the compound, and three of us went down. We left work early. The compound was massive; it was an aerospace compound, and they had their supermarket. That was great. We took our gear to our rooms, went to the supermarket, and each went in with three different trolleys without speaking to each other. I got sugar and grape juice by the caseload with baker's yeast by the box. The other lads were doing the same, but they were also putting 5-gallon bins in the truck. We left at different times, but we got them into the truck. We then had to go to the big cheese who had a team of Filipinos who distilled the Sidiki, and we were never to find out where. We phoned him up and were told to be there at 7 o'clock, and no later. We got a taxi from the compound to his house.

It was a mansion with 2 guard dogs at the front and a guard. We had a meeting, he knew we were turning up. He opened these large gates and took us inside to meet him. He called himself Dave, although I don't think that was his proper name. He introduced us to his wife, who was a stunner. We were taken to the film room, which had 20-plus chairs and a big screen. I had seen nothing like it. He had a servant who gave us Sid. We relaxed our guard as he told us what he did and how he was well connected with a prince who got containers full of whiskey into the country. Dave used to buy it, and deals were done with backhanders to get the stuff in. This Dave was making big money. He would not say where he came from in England, but his wife asked where I came from. I said Hyde, and she was about to say where she came from, but Dave shut her up, and she changed the conversation.

We got on about deals he was doing with our big boss on-site. He said, "You know the blue flame?" I said, "Yes." He said, "When the

Sid arrives, you do the blue flame, and if it's yellow, you let me know and get the distillers fucked for supplying shitty stuff. People have gone blind by drinking shite Sid." He said, "From now on when you come down to the compound, this phone number I am going to give you, ring it, and just tell them where your truck is. They will give you a time they will be there. Give them the money, and 5 gallons will be put in the truck. End off. Don't say anything, don't tell them anything. Then, Saturday morning, have breakfast, then get up the road to Tanajib before the roads get busy. If you get caught, don't mention me or you will never see home again." I thought, "Fuck me right over my head here." He then said, "Right, lads, thanks and goodbye. May see you again or I may not."

We got a taxi back to the compound, phoned the number, and told him the reg number and compound and hutch number. The guy said someone would be there in 20 minutes. Two guys arrived in a truck, found us no problem, asked for the money, we gave it to them, and they never checked it. They put 5 gallons in the back of the truck, we would do the blue flame when we got back to Tanajib. We then found one of the bars and got shit-faced.

The next morning, the three of us were hungover. I was unable to drive and was vomiting, so my boss drove 4 hours journey back. I slept all the way there. We put all the gear in the lock-up, and I said, "We'd best test the Sid we got." We got a spoon and poured some of the Sid from the 5-gallon water bottle it was in. We lit it and, bingo, a blue flame. The Sid was okay. By the time we got our shit sorted, it was lunchtime, and we had a bloody good swim at the pool before the evening meal. Then I wrote a letter home and went to bed, ready to return to work on Saturday.

On the work side, we were starting to strip one of the gas compressors. My boss used to say, "Today we will strip this piece, and that's it." I went to the lads and told them, "That's as far as we go for today." But his logic was good: "We will spend more time on the job." By this time, we were about a month into the job, and I still had three months left before going on R&R to spend two weeks with Sue. At this time in my marriage, things were getting a bit strained, but I can now tell you that we are very happy. You have to work on a marriage like anything else in life. We worked on it, and now we've been married for over 40 years, and the last 5 have been the best. I am diversifying now, so I will get back to the bar.

We have been very busy over the past 3 weeks. The road where all the heavy drinkers were staying, we called it "Swally Alley." The bar was something like an English pub. In the back was the brewing room. By now, we had bottles with stoppers for the wine, which we had in red and white. It was not bad at all. For beer, we had over 100 bottles ready for serving and 15 gallons of Sid. So, we decided to have the opening of the bar on a Thursday evening, the start of the weekend. The three of us finished work early to get everything ready for the 5 o'clock opening. We got everything ready for our first opening.

The first lads to get in were "The Growler" and his mate, "The Jock." These two, we found out, were alcoholics. We all liked a drink, but these two were professional drinkers. These two would be a pain for us over the coming years. They came in and asked for Sid and Marander. That would be their stamp. I put more in than I should have done. The Growler brought in his guitar and put it over the bar to look after it. After the first hour, we got busy. People were drinking the beer and wine by the gallon like they had never seen the stuff before. As the night got going, so did the lads. Around 8 pm, The Growler was drunk with his sidekick. He now wanted his guitar. By this time of the night, he was well pissed. He started to play all Elvis songs. He could not sing, but we were all drunk, so it sounded okay. As the night went on, the more he thought he was Elvis. Fucking hell, trying to stop him from singing was hard. He stopped playing and then fucked off to bed. I thought we would have trouble with this fucker, you guessed it we did or should I say I did.

The first night turned out to be a good night. We made money. On the first week, we had enough money to get a 45-inch TV. That was a big TV back then. The second week, we had a music centre, which I took home 2 years later.

On the work front, the first gas compressor we were going to strip was a split-level compressor. The top came off and the rotor taken out, but lifting the top off was prone to disaster if not done right. There were around 50 4-inch stud bolts holding the top on, but you had to have a vertical lift or you would take the threads off the stud bolts, and the lead time for new was 2 years. Not an option to get it wrong, so I thought about it, and this took me 48 hrs. and no sleep thinking about it. One night it came to me at about 3 am how to do it, and it was to get 8 chain blocks attached to the crane and to the steel straps which were on top of the lid. Put 2 spirit levels on both sides, crack the seal with the crane, then level up the top with the chain blocks, keep it level with the spirit levels. Once level, slowly raise it with the 50-ton crane which we had on-site. And hey, presto, it worked. Backslapping was the order of the day and a good drink at night.

On gas compressors, here is what a gas compressor does in an oil plant. Petrochemical plants covert feedstocks produced from crude oil refining and natural gas processing into usable products like ethylene and propylene. Ariel rotor compressors which we had both on-site, basically compressed the gas which came off the oil and sent it down the line to the gas plant and oil to the oil terminal down in Ras Tanura. The 2 types of gas compressors I had on-site were reciprocating and axial compressors. Gas compressors are used in various applications where either higher pressure or lower volumes of gas are needed in the pipeline transport of purified natural gas from the production site to the consumer. We were on-site, compressed the gas, and stored it in great big vessels before sending it down the line.

YOU ONLY LOSE WHAT YOU CLING TO

Getting back to the bar, we had been trading for a few months, and everything was going okay. It was my turn to go down to Korbar one

Thursday night to pick up 5 gallons of Sid. I left early and was down there by 6 pm. I went to the big house, rang the bell, and the wife came to the gates. She said he is not here and didn't know when he would be back. She then went back inside. I then went and checked into our compound, went to the bar, asked a few questions, and found out he had been arrested for smuggling guns into the country. We were messing about with some weird shit out here. They told me to keep my head down up in Tanajib; there could be some more collateral coming. On a good note, they said we could buy Sid from them, but it was more expensive. So, I paid them, had a few drinks, put the booze in the truck, had an early night, and set off up the road to camp.

We did find out his wife went missing, and the big house got boarded up. We never got to the bottom of it, but we did find out he was smuggling everything into the country. He had contacts with royalty who were not to be trusted. Did they kill them? I will never know, but the bar was stocked up once again and making money. The first year came and went. I spent Christmas over there, which was a fucking good piss-up, to say the least. We used to get lads coming in from offshore who would have spent 4 months on an oil rig. These fuckers, you would know they were offshore workers because they had a 1000-yard stare, being cooped up on a small platform. The only exercise was on the Heli deck.

The first month there, Brenden and I went to look at Khafji. It was where Saddam broke through into Saudi but was turned back by the Yanks. The Saudis like to make you think they did it, but it was the Yanks. We got to the outskirts of Khafji only to find a city blown to pieces. There was nothing left. The Yanks must have pounded it to the ground. I looked at what I thought was a water tower, but it was the elevator shaft of high-rise flats. You would not believe what war can do, and later on in Gulf War 2, I would be there, but there was plenty of water to go under the bridge before getting there.

Back on the job front, I went home on RR after 4 months for a 2-week break. I arrived home with a 1000-yard stare and a yearning to get out, which sent me on a 2-week piss-up. This life was not for a family man. My biggest regret is that I should have known better, but all I wanted to do was go on the piss. Bad move and it still haunts me to this day - a very selfish man. But I was doing it for a reason, to get back up the ladder. But what I know now is that money is not everything. I shall take those bad memories to my grave if only.

MONEY IS THE ROOT OF ALL EVIL

Well, my time to go back was here again. As I said, I used to go to the airport on my own, leaving Sue at home. The last record we used to hear was "Leaving on a Jet Plane." Once I arrived at the airport, I switched on my work head to tackle another 4 months in that shit hole of a desert. Same thing, arrived at Skipol airport to pick my main flight to Saudi but stopped off at the main bar to speak to other expats going to different parts of the Middle East. It was like a breath of fresh air talking to people on the same wavelength as me.

I got into Saudi around 9 pm and got out of the terminal around 11 pm, to be picked up and taken to our compound for the night. The next morning, I got my clearance papers, handed back my passport, and picked up my truck. Then, I headed up to Tanajib. I used to take my time getting up there. I knew I had 4 months of shite going on, and when you fucked up, it was still there the next day. I had plenty of sleepless nights thinking about how to get the job done, but like everything in life, the job always gets done by hook or by crook. Plus, we were still running the bar.

The bar was going from strength to strength. People were going home on leave and bringing things back for the bar. But there was one day when things went tits up. The Growler was on the piss all day in his room, then decided to come into the bar. Before he came into the bar, he fell out with 2 Yanks whom he twatted, and both were sparked out. Unknown to me, I did not know what happened till I served him a double Sid. We then heard a bit of a scuffle at the door. These 2

Yanks wanted to slot him, so it started off in the bar. We got it under control, but Growler was still on one. I said to him, "What the fuck's going on, you fucking moron?" He took a swing and missed me, but the glass he had in his hand broke on the bar. I smacked him; then the glass got stuck into my little finger. Claret everywhere needed stitching, but being pissed, I could not go to the hospital. I would be arrested. So one of the lads closed the cut with butterfly plasters and said, "You'll have to go to the hospital tomorrow." By this time, the bar was shut, the 2 Yanks went home, and Growler was still pissed but was taken home. We then closed the bar.

The next day, I went to the hospital and told them I did it in the sink while washing glasses. I had 4 stitches put in. Then, the doctor said I needed an injection, but I told him I was allergic to penicillin. Despite my allergy, I was still given an injection. Five minutes later, I was in pain. My head swelled up, and my feet were like red hot coals. I went straight back to the doctor who gave me another injection and said to go home and not go to work for 2 days. I thought, "hay ho," but I was feeling like shit. When I got back to my room, I went to bed. At dinner time, some of the lads came to see me. The 2 Yanks were on their way home. Growler got a warning, but there was a big meeting by Fluor Daniel in the afternoon to explain what happened. I was feeling like shit, but the lads helped me to the site and the meeting room. I had a great big bandage on my hand and was bandaged on my arm. My head swelled up. The big cheese came in, looked at me, and said, "What the fuck happened?" I said I did not know, only that it kicked off. The bottom line was that the bar would close for 1 month on the strength of it. At least no Brit was sent home, but my finger does not work anymore. I must have severed a ligament. I'm still here to tell the tale, another battle wound which I have many over the years, being a warrior at the edge of time and saying things which are the truth, and some people do not like it.

The time was zooming by. I started working 7 days a week, so that stopped me from going down to Dharan, which was good. But the bad thing was when I was on leave; I was going to the pub at least for the first week. This put a big strain on our marriage. Women today would not take the crap I gave Susan and the kids. I knew when I went back it was four months of shite, but we are into our 2nd year and things on site are going well.

The first compressor we worked on was nearly finished; it just needed to be flushed out. That meant flushing the miles of pipe work out with hot oil, which we heated with the heaters in the sump of the machine and diverted the oil to go around the system. Every 100 yds or so, we had very fine screens fitted to catch any crap that was in the system (which there was a lot), and it had to be crystal clear for when we hooked it back to the compressor. Any shit would foul and stop the compressor when online, and you did not want that. So, we had an inspector check the oil flush every 24 hours.

When this process was completed, we then pumped the 24 barrels of oil to the next compressor. We did this during lunchtime, and I told one of the lads to watch the transfer of oil while we went for lunch. When we came back, the Indian said, "Mr. Peter, oil went there, but not there; it disappeared." "Fuck me," I said. We found a valve that was passing, but where did the oil go? That was the problem. We went to a pit where waste oil should have gone, but there was nothing there.

This was an environmental problem. We were next to the sea, so is it going into the sea or into the desert? Both were bad. I had to go and tell the bosses. Shit hit the fan; the company would be fined or even thrown out of the country if this got out. So it was "mum's the word." We even got a small boat to go up and down to see if there was any oil slick, but after 2 days, we knew we were in the clear. But where it went, no one knows to this day. Happy days.

After 2 years, the bar was closed for good. There had been too many fights, etc., so the management had no option but to close it. I was not bothered, really. I just drank in my room. But I will say I had some very bad hangovers in the 2 plus years I was out there and lost days and nights, one of which came back to haunt me.

There was a bloke who thought he was Irish and believed in the IRA. One night in the bar, just about to close, he was spouting off about the IRA. He got on my nerves, and I one-arrowed him. When he woke up, he said to my mate, "Did you see him do that?" Next thing, Bren twatted him. He was a wanker, but a strange thing happened. He went on leave but never came back. A few months down the line, we got a message that he had never reached home, but his passport was found in London. Did he open his mouth to someone when pissed about the IRA? One will never know.

As I said from the beginning, this job lasted for 3 years. When I went back for the last tour of duty, we commissioned the plant, and all my compressors worked a bloody miracle. We opened the bar for one last time, had a good piss-up, and we all started to drift off to other jobs. I went offshore in Rastanura for 1 month, flying out every day. I was stopping at a camp not far from the heliport. I was the second man from our firm on this compound, so we were all going to be put next to each other so we could have a drink at night together. Well, I met this chap who I thought was odd, but we were all a bit odd to be out there and stay at home. Got talking to him, and he was saying he was out all through Gulf War One and seeing Scuds dropping into Dharan. I was a bit jealous, to be honest. Well, after a few drinks, he brought out of his hooch a silver tin hat he had chromed, but that was not all. Next drink, he went into his room and came out as an American officer with all the uniform pressed. It looked new. He then sat down and opened his top pocket, and out came a cigarette holder. He put a cig in it and started to talk like nothing was wrong. Well, I couldn't hold myself. I said, "You look great, bro. Do you dress like that often?" "At least once a month," he replied. Mmm, I thought, "This some weird fucker." But he was supplying the drink, so I did not say anything else. Went to bed pissing myself. Well, in a couple of weeks, we had 6 of us stopping on site, and yes, I did tell the lads. And yes, one night, he came out dressed as the officer. That would be the last time he did. The piss was taken literally.

Nothing much was happening, really. Only, I did like flying out every day to the rig but did not really do much. It was a holding place for me. It came to a head when the boss of the rig said it's costing too much to keep flying you out every day, so I will have to let you go. So, I had a week to Christmas and should be going home the first week of January, spending another Christmas in Saudi. So, thinking they would finish me and send me home for Christmas, I was told to go down to the empty quarter, a 5-hour journey. I got there, and the superintendent who I knew from way back, said there is no job here for you. Your boss wants you to do Christmas here and new year and then finish your contract. The reason is you hit him one night in the bar in his compound. Now, I knew the Sid was strong shit, but I didn't and still don't know I hit him. But I will tackle him when I fly out. My flight was booked for the 3rd of Jan. I spent a shite Christmas and new year in a hovel of a hotel and was really shafted. I met a guy on Christmas Eve; he was on jankers as well. We had no booze, fuck all, but it turned out to be a good time.

This lad was well up in the Catholic Church, or should I say he was. He talked about how the Jesuits who are an apostolic religious community called the society of Jesus took the Gestapo out of Germany and how they knew about the Jews and were in cohorts with Hitler. Well, that was Christmas. New year was the same. Then, it was time to fly home for the last time. When I got back to the main office in Dammam, the boss was still on leave. I was going to give him a fucking good bollocking, but he knew I was finished, so he had an extra week in the UK so he would not meet me, fucking wimp. So, I headed home to plan my next adventure.

LIFE IS FOR LIVING; YOU JUST HAVE ONE SHOT AT IT

I came home and tried to get back into a routine like other normal families, but it was not the case for me. Susan had a routine. With our children encouraging there interest e.g. swimming dancing cricket. I now regret not taking much interest in it but now I can not get that back. Susan had sorted her life out with her friends, while I had drifted away from mine. So, it was time to look for another job in the Middle East. It came through Brendan, who was working in Syria. He called me up and said to change my CV to include more about gas engines, and he would get me a job out there. So, I doctored my CV and had a phone interview with one of the directors, who was a woman that later became a good friend down the line. I got the job, so I packed in the job I had, which was an installation firm where I was putting big presses at a place in Burnley. I played "Leaving on a Jet Plane" and left Susan at home like I always did. I got into the taxi and then changed to be an oilman. I had to get my head on board for this job.

I arrived at Schiphol Airport, when to the bar before catching the plane to Damascus. I had a few drinks and got talking with a few expats who were going to different places in the Middle East. It was a nice leveller. When I landed in Damascus, I went to the office, got sorted with them, and then they took me to the bus station. They put me on a bus and said it would take 4 to 5 hours. "Fuck me; where the hell was I going?" I was going to a place called Deir ez-Or on the Iraq border.

I arrived in Deir ez-Or after a stop in Palmira, which is a old Roman city. On the hills, there are Christian forts which the Christian Crusaders used while on their way to Jerusalem. Now most of it is destroyed by ISIS. Here was halfway; many times, I would be stopping here during my 3 years of working in this police state, another country with more guns than people, but that's for later.

When I arrived, I was taken to my room to drop my gear off. It was a 20-man dorm where you had your own room and toilet. I found out we were subbed out to Shell. The Shell lads were at the top end, and us contractors were at the bottom. I've been in worse digs. I was then taken to the site around a mile down the road. I looked at the plant and realized this was not Saudi. The plant was run down, and the oil reserves were coming to a close. There were nodding donkeys all over the desert, meaning the oil reserves were not free-flowing. They had to inject water down the wells, which mixed with the oil and the nodding donkeys. Then they pumped up the oil and water, which went to a GOSP, a process that took oil from the water, and the gas was used to run the gas engines on the plant, which I was a part of.

I went to meet my boss and his sidekick, well, same thing as my last job. These guys had done their bit and had enough, so they were just telling me how bad it was here, but I knew different. The lads took me to meet my workforce, which was all Syrians and Indians. Seemed a good bunch. First day was over, then back to the room. Knock on the door; one of our lads said we are having a drink tonight for you, so would you like to go into town for a bottle, which I said no problem. Went into town and found this off-license which the man who owned it knew the lads, so I got a bottle of gin. My mate said, "You may need more, just in case we don't come back for a while." So, I bought 4 bottles, which I thought should last me for the 8 weeks I will be there before RR, not so I was to find out. We got back to base and had an evening meal; then I went to another lad's room, where I met 5 of us who were not Shell. There were 5 on leave at the moment, so we all finished together and went on leave, which I thought was good, and the first trip, I was only going to do 7 weeks to fit into the groove. Better still, so we had a fucking good night, nothing much left of my gin, though, plus I had a fucking head in the morning. I believe we were singing till 12 o'clock when the Shell lads came down and told us to shut the party down. I then found out it was them and us for the next three years.

The primary function of a tree is to control the flow, usually oil or gas, out of the well. A tree may also be used to control the injection of gas or water into a non-producing well in order to enhance production rates of oil from other wells. When the well and facilities are ready to produce and receive oil or gas, tree valves are opened, and the formation fluids are allowed to go through a flow line. This leads to a processing facility, storage depot, and/or other pipeline eventually leading to a refinery or Distribution centre back to back (for gas). Flow lines on subsea wells usually lead to a fixed or floating production platform or to a storage ship or barge, known as a floating storage offloading vessel (FSO), or floating processing unit (FPU), or floating production, storage and offloading vessel (FPSO).

A tree often provides numerous additional functions, including chemical injection points, well intervention means, pressure relief means, monitoring points (such as pressure, temperature, corrosion, erosion, sand detection, flow rate, flow composition, valve and choke position feedback), and connection points for devices such as downhole pressure and temperature transducers (DHPT). On producing wells, chemicals, alcohols, or oil distillates may be injected to preclude production problems, such as blockages.

One of my biggest jobs, where I did not have a clue how to start or finish it, was a great bi-gas diesel engine - a superior 12-cylinder. It was as big as a house and one of six that ran the plant and gave electricity to the site. The thing with this one was one of the cylinder liners needed changing - a mammoth job in 120-degree heat and 140 degrees when the rest of the engines were working. First, I had to do some research. This took me a couple of days. I then purchased the liner from Damascus, which I hope would arrive for my back to back to do when I was on leave. No such luck. It arrived 2 months later when I had just arrived back from RR. Shit. My men and I were tasked to do it. You have a load of paperwork to do to take it offline and put blind flanges on the incoming and outgoing pipe work. We had a timescale of three days to do it, or else there would be ramifications down in Damascus from head office.

So, this liner was the size for size of the cylinder wall. In this heat, the bloody thing would expand and would get stuck, and we would be in a world of shit. So, I purchased a big freezer from Deir ez-Or, which is the nearest town. We got it set up near the job site and put this liner in it for 3 days. On the third day, we started to take the piston out, which was around 4 feet long. We did this on the night shift. The day shift took out the old liner. We had the tools for the job, but it took 12 hours of struggling.

In the morning, I measured the bore and then the outside diameter of the liner. It was 0.010" smaller, which means it should just piss in. We then brought the fridge up to the generator, put on gloves, brought the crane over, attached the top end, and lifted it into position. We dropped it in. By this time, it was getting warmer, but it finally went in without any problem. This was thinking on your feet. In 2 days, it was back online, running a bit rough, but the job was done, and a pat on the back for the team and me. If you have a good team, it makes you look good. Always remember that. If you fall out with your team some way down the road, they will fuck you over. Another thing to remember: you have to be confident in all that you do in life because when we feel confident in ourselves, we are able to trust in our own abilities, qualities, and judgment.

Now, at the time I was there, it was the father of the leader who now runs Syria. He was a tyrant, like his son. He ran the country from 1971 to 2000. When I was there, the military intelligence service, or the Mukhabarat in Arabic, was very influential in Syrian politics and was, and is, controlled by President past and present Bashar. The service also monitors opponents of the government outside of Syria. So, to say we had secret police in our office is not an understatement. The locals were afraid of speaking to us in case they got arrested, which a few did. The only way I could speak to the locals was when I took them out into the desert to unmanned sites like pumping stations. Then they would to talk about the shit that was going on in the country. The president always won the elections; it was won by the gun.

When I was taking four lads on a job into the dessert one of them told me about his brother. He was arrested in the town square for talking about the president. This resulted in him going to jail for 6 months before his trial. When he got to court, he was found guilty, which was inevitable. He got 4 years, but they did not send him down for the 4 years. Instead, they sent the breadwinner of the household to an underground prison which the lad who was telling me had mentioned. The prison held 2000 people. When I got home (not at work because your computer was tapped), I emailed a letter to the authorities, which I had saved. I got a reply 6 months later stating, "Yes, we do know about the prison. It's a funny old world, isn't it?"

Another two strange things whilst I was there. We were all working in the office, and no one was on site that date when 2 lads collapsed on the floor. An ambulance came and rushed them to the hospital. Then, another lad dropped to the floor. And then it happened to me; I just collapsed on the floor like a ton of spuds. I was taken to the hospital, and while going through the ward, I saw the first two lads sitting on the edge of a bed. I was not in a fit state to speak to them. They got me in this room, and the doctor said, "I think I know what it is. I will give you a shot, and you will feel better." I turned around, and I saw him pick a needle out of a tray. I just had enough strength to say, "Fuck off! I want a new needle!" He said I would be charged for it, but at that time, I did not give a fuck. After he injected me, in 10 minutes, I was as right as rain, and so were the other 3. To this day, we never got to the bottom of what it was, but someone knew.

The next thing to happen was that there was a guy who had chronic pains. He then passed a three-foot-long worm, put it in a bottle of gin, and took it home on RR to find out what the hell it was. When he came back, he told us all that this was very common around there. We all went to the hospital and told them this story, and they agreed. They gave everyone on site a tablet to take. From that day we took the tablets on a regular monthly basis. You would not credit it would you?

I spent two Christmases away from home in the three years I was there. Syria is, and still is, a fucked-up country run by a tyrant family and run by the gun. Hangings were a weekly treat on a Friday in the football stadium. We knew how many were going to be hanged by the number of cranes they were. They just put a rope around their neck and pulled them off the ground, so they strangled to death. Fucking barbaric.

2 more incidents happened while in Syria one of the directors came to visit us on site unannounced she was called Esmee

I turned a corner and bumped in to her realising. Who it was I said, "You are the one with the sexy voice". She then said "I may have a sexy voice but my looks don't match" my reply was "Anything looks better than a camel after 8 weeks" she had good communications with so she told her what I said she respected her workforce and kept inclosed contact with the family's.

The last Christmas there we had a big party with all other oil refinerys around we being the nearest got there first by the time the last group got there we were well pissed. The first act was a belly dancer where once she started I jumped on stage and tried to do the same somehow ever we both collided and fell of the stage where upon she said to everyone she is taking her troup of dancers back to Damascus then all hell broke loose cans of beer were flying across to me.

I thought they would lynch me but it got squared away by Esmee and the show went on and a good night by all.

I left Syria on a high, thinking I was going straight back into a job in the Middle East after a good break. It was not to be, but my next main adventure was my best time and a fucking good earner. As the saying goes, "Stand outside a barber's shop and one day, you will get a haircut."

REMEMBER YOU ONLY GET ONE SHOT IN THIS LIFE SO TAKE IT, ITS BETTER TO LIVE LIKE A LION FOR 20 YEARS THAN 40 YEARS AS A SHEEP.

My homecoming was the same, no big thing. Dad's back home and spent a couple of weeks on the piss. Then I thought, time to get a job. But as I was thinking this, my old mate Brendon Spirren from Spennymoor phoned me. He told me he was dying and that this would be the last time we spoke together. The next time would be in Valhalla. We said our goodbyes, and he said it was going to be him or me, given the amount of drink we had consumed over the years. Yes, three years running a bar in Saudi and three years in Syria. I wouldn't take those years back, but I might have been a better husband and father. At the time, you think you are unbeatable, but cancer has other ideas. We said our goodbyes, and I never heard from him again.

So, I started looking for a job back in the UK. I found a job at a firm called WFEL, which was once Fairy Engineering in Stockport. WFEL was and still is a global leader in tactical military bridges, supplying over 40 armed forces around the world for more than four decades. One of the new products I was going to be a part of was the DSB (Dry Support Bridge). An overview of the DSB is that just eight soldiers and a single launch vehicle can get traffic moving over a 46-meter gap in less than 90 minutes using the DSB. The DSB is still the leading rapidly deployable military bridge of its kind in the world. It is used in both military and disaster relief operations. The DSB is in operation with the American, Swiss, Australian, and Turkish armies. The DSB can span a 46-meter gap in under 90 minutes. Its primary mission is to be emplaced on main supply routes in the rear of the area of direct combat.

I went for an interview and got the job. With my expertise working in far-flung places, the company had only just made the prototype, and now they were in production over 100 for the Yanks.

I started on a wet and windy Monday morning. Being what I am like, I arrived early and met a guy who would be in the same bay as me, making the launch frame, and I was going to manufacture the slide frame. The superintendent came along and introduced me to the supervisor called, Tim. I took a dislike to him from the start. I thought this did not bode well.

I started to get into the job it did not take me long to realise everyone was in the same boat. No one knew what they were doing at the time they were all chances? and they had only made one prototype. As the weeks went on, there were people sacked on a weekly level. Some did not have a clue, so I got my head down and tried to be a grey man, but that does not last long when you are like me, who sees something and that is not right I will my say. We all worked on building it on the shop floor.

The supervisor was getting on my tits. He thought he was better than the rest of us because he was a toolmaker and a fucking tool at that. I had been there for around 6 months, and me and this lad had fuck all to do, so we went to the superintendent and told him we had no work, where in turn he went to our supervisor and told him the situation. This did not go down well with him. He found a shit job for both of us. After 2 days, my mate was going to leave. I told him the same money for doing shite, and when you are marching, you are not fighting, meaning we cannot fuck up what we are doing.

In the afternoon, this Tim came in and said, "You don't fuck with me. I am your boss. Next time I will sack you." So, in a rage, I pulled him behind the screens and told him some home truths about his mother and wife. "The only thing you can do to me is send me home to my wife and kids," I said. It's funny what a bollocking can do. The next day we were put back on the DSB. He did not speak to me for weeks, which did not bother me. After around 6 months, the second DSB was coming to completion. There were 4 main parts, and these were large parts: the slide frame which was mine, the A-frame, and the launch frame, and all this went on to an Oshkosh truck. We all worked on stripping it down and putting new bits on to take all this tackle on. This process was new to us all; it had never been done in the workshop before. They were trying times. When we finally got this lot together, which took us 4 weeks, which we can now do in 2 days, it was time to make the bridge itself. We had another team for that, but we did help to build me putting spacers in between the panels, measuring them, and fitting them. This will bite us in the Ares months later. We now had to commission the truck before we took it outside to build a bridge. This took 2 weeks with oil leaks etc., trying times. The director was on the shop floor all day; his reputation stood on this working properly. If he did not like your face, he would get you sacked. He took a shine to me. I was the grey man around him, he did not want to come out with bullshit, and he could see straight through it. By this time, the design team was all over the truck like a rash, finding things they had done wrong. We were the grunts who had to put things right, but this is heavy engineering, not a morning's job to strip something and replace it with new. So, the truck took around six to get it outside and trial it. The Yanks wanted this yesterday. We did a build with it. Only one inspection said it was good to go. My thoughts were not properly commissioned. This is going to bite us on our arse. So, they shipped it to the USA.

Now the Yanks wanted four at a time for each base, so this truck stayed in America for 8 months until the other 3 were finished. Then a team of our lads would go over there and teach them how to use it. I was not one of those people; they knew I could build the fuckers. They thought I was winging it, as well as the rest. By the second year, we got into the swing of things. Tim, the supervisor, was sacked; a fucking wanker. I could have had him sacked earlier. We had a team from another company doing a night shift. This Tim told them to mark out and drill for these big blocks, which they did and fucked up. We used to put the block on the frame and drill through so the holes would be in line. What this crew did over a 4-night spell was go back to their company, offset the holes to fit, bushed them, and no one knew. I was told 5 years later bu. But years down the line, it came back for refurbishment, and then no one ever spotted it, only me.

Then came 9/11. This was to change my life forever. They were sending a bridge to Iraq and wanted people to go. I said I would go. Two other lads went first and went to Iraq. I was sent to Fort Bliss, Texas, for weapons and survival training. So off I go. I get to the base after flying down to El Paso. They picked me up from the airport. I showed them my orders, and I was sent to a barracks. I was the first there, so over the day, it got full. There were squaddies, ex-squaddies, and contractors, each given a different barrack. Well, at 1800 hrs, we were all called to the parade ground and put into line. In that week we were going to cover some important information what and not to do and what to look out for in theatre (war zone). It started "wheels up in 7 days." I thought mmmm, must be a Yank thing. We were told we should be going into classes over the week for survival to see if someone was going to do suicide, a big thing in the USA army. So we then got told the CIA would be on campus. Do not talk to them, and they may be on one of your courses. I said to my new mate, "How the fuck do you know who they are?" He said, "You will," and that was that. I could not sleep the first night, thinking this was great stuff, a man's world.

The first day was medical. I had 3 teeth sorted out. You don't want tooth problems in a war zone. Then it was injection time. Fuck me, 8 injections. One of them was a live type, and they said if you touch it with your fingers, it will spread over your body. They gave us pictures of people who had touched their faces and lips. Fuck me, what the fuck are they giving us? After going forward 3 years, I went to the doctors with my medical card to see what injections I needed for a holiday in Kenya with Susan They kept the card because they did not know what two of the injections were for when I went back for a booster they returned my card and said "We do not know what the two injections were for", I said fuck me what did they pump into me now going back to the course as the week progress music was played every day and everyday was wheels up in 5 days counting down.

This was some sort of trick to get you hyped up. Then, there was a situation in the main hall when the CIA arrived. In the same meeting, they sat on one side of the room. I told my new mate, "I am going to sit with them." He said, "Pete, do not go sit with them. They are a different breed of people." Like a cunt, I went over and sat with them. I was told in no uncertain way, "Go fuck yourself and go and sit over there." These fuckers meant it. I duly went back, and my mate said, "You don't fuck with those guys. They can really fuck your day up." So, no more. I kept a low profile from that day on. It was on a Wednesday when we went on a 9mm pistol shooting and then a night shoot. I thought, "This is the dog's bollocks. I will be carrying a 9mm with me. Fucking great shit."

On a Friday morning, we all got a call to muster on the parade ground. Names were read out for those who would not fly out on Saturday. My name was one because I did not have a visa in my passport. I was told to stand down and get back to my company. I was devastated. One guy said, "Don't worry. Come and work for us when you get back give us a ring money in it for you." But this did not help. They build you up to a pitch and then just let you down without any help. I bugged out in a hotel and cried all night that I could not fly out with the team I had been with all week. It was some kind of mind control they had on you for that week. Without me knowing, I had two injections which I knew fuck all about. I still do not know what the fuck they gave me. But one thing I do know: my fuse had shortened since having it. When I have a drink, it goes straight to my head, and I lose control, become a right twat.

So, on that night, I got a taxi and went into Al Paso and got storming drunk. I finished in this club with some of the lads from the base. We all got steaming drunk, but they were going out to Iraq the following afternoon. Lucky bastards. I phoned work the next day, and they told me to send my passport over and sit in the hotel until it arrived back with a stamp on it. I told them, "I am not stopping with no passport in America. What happens if I got pulled over with the law?" So, I got a plane back to the UK with a business card for Worley Parsons, who had a contract with the USA government.

I got home and I phoned the number I was given. I was told to send my CV over and wait for a callback. I went back to work and told them I was not interested in going back, and that was that. My mate, who was in Iraq, had to wait another month before flying home. I don't think he and his family ever forgave me for it, but I was out to look after myself and my family.

It was around 3 weeks later that I got a phone call and an interview. The interview was on the phone, which I liked because you can bullshit a bit better over the phone. They wanted a mechanical engineer. Fuck me, you need a fucking degree for that position, but I bullshitted the interview. After the interview, I was told that if I accepted the role, I would be working outside of the wire and that I might get blown up, killed, or captured. The salary would be massive. I didn't want to sound overjoyed, so I asked if there were any other perks. Fuck me; part of my gas and electricity would be paid for in the UK, all expenses paid, and a loyalty bonus as well. I said yes to those terms, and the rest is history.

I received a letter with my orders for Iraq, but first, I had to go to the embassy in London for my warrant card, which would let me into Kuwait and army bases without showing my passport. But as you will see, we don't know what was going on in this country. I took the train down first class, all paid for. When I got to the embassy, I asked the guard where to go. He then asked for my orders. He told me to just go around the corner, and I would see what I needed. It was a very strange thing to say, but I thought nothing of it. Not thinking anything of it, I walked all the way down to the bottom as far as I could go. Then, I turned around, and there was a guy in civilian clothes playing with the door. He must have been the security of the embassy. He approached me and asked for my orders. After he checked them, he opened the garage door, which was full of cars. I thought it was very strange. We walked a few hundred yards into this place, and we came to a lift shaft.

He did something, which I cannot now remember, and then the doors opened. He said, "Don't touch anything; stay still, and when the doors open, someone will be waiting for you." I stepped in. I don't know if the lift went up or down. When the doors opened, in front of me was a man dressed in Navy uniform well it looked like it to me. He said, "Mr. Oldham, orders, please." He looked at them and said, "Follow me." We went into this large office where everyone was wearing a Naval uniform. It was bloody strange, I thought. Then, we went into this small office, and he said, "Take a seat." He started logging down my details. After around 15 minutes, he said, "Done. We shall go for a coffee, and you should have your warrant card, i.e., kak card." I asked, "What's happening now?" He said, "It's going through your family's history to see if there are any bad guys in it." I said, "I am English, and you are American." He said categorically, "It does not work like that, Mr. Oldham." So, I shut my mouth and went for coffee. I came back around 20 minutes later, and it was done. What shit do the Yanks have on, us brits but hay ho, I am on my way home. I left as I came in, went to the nearest pub, had a meal, three pints, and a taxi back to the station. I was a really happy bunny. I got on the train and slowly got pissed. These were going to be or sometimes. I reached home a little pissed, told Suzan how I went on, and said it's just a waiting game now for the ticket to Iraq or first Kuwait, then Iraq. I went to work on Monday, said my goodbyes, which I don't like, and slipped out unnoticed. I did not want to make a big deal about it.

I went home, a little low leaving the firm I got used to, but soon cheered up thinking of the money I was going to be on. Not that I could get killed in a jot or blinded, that would be worse, and that haunted me for the 2 years I was there. But this was going to be the culminating point in my life. I have made it - MECHANICAL ENGINEER, no degree, albeit no one else wanted the job, fucking wimps. You don't get anywhere without taking risks. Better to live like a lion for 10 years than 40 years a sheep.

I started getting my shit together for my big adventure. As I said before, stand outside a barber's shop long enough, and you will get a haircut. Little did I know there was more to the job than meets the eye. I was getting paid for being at home, not bad, I thought.

Then the day came. I got a phone call from the states - "Get to the airport tomorrow, wheels up 10 am to Kuwait, then someone will meet you, take you to a hotel till morning. Then either you will fly into Kirkuk or drive into Basra. This will be decided by operations on the day. You are now signed up with the American military as a contractor, and you are under general order number 1 - no drink, no going with the other sex, etc. etc. etc." I got all this with my paperwork and orders, which came a few days before, so I knew what to expect.

The big day came. I played "Leaving on a Jet Plane" for the last time and said my farewells to Susan on the doorstep. As the taxi came to pick me up, my mood changed. Now, I am on my own. I collected my thoughts and got on with the job in question. I arrived at the airport and went to the bar. There, I chatted to a couple of guys who were going to Saudi. I told them it's a shit hole and they will be treated like third-class citizens. I warned them about all the bullshit about booze and how I ran a bar over there. I advised them not to get involved with anything. Then, they asked about me. I told them where I was going and who I was working for. I got a little big-headed, but it didn't take long for me to start thinking, "What the fuck have I got myself into?" Then, I thought, "Well, this is what I have been waiting for all these years. It's the icing on the cake."

COWADS DIE MANY TIMES BEFORE THEIR DEATHS THE VALIENT NEVER TASTE OF DEATH ONLY ONCE

I left the bar, walking the slow march down to the waiting room to get on my flight. This is it, I thought; no turning back now. They asked for seats 59 to 100, that's it, off I go. I settled in on the plane, wheels up, and now there was no turning back. How many times have I done this before, and how many more times will I be doing it? Will I survive out of the wire? All this was crossing my mind.

It was time for a drink, and the stewardess came round. Double Baileys and Brandy was the first and last drink on the flight. With what I had at the bar and this last drink, I was gone. I missed my food and woke up with one hour to go before touch down. Bloody hell. They came around with the departure forms to fill in. By the time I got a pen, we were coming into land. Fuck me; we are in Kuwait. How am I going to get into Iraq? By road or plane? Anyhow, I had to spend six hours in a hotel before leaving for Iraq. As a Mechanical Engineer, will I be able to do the job? Fuck knows. I will play the grey man, say fuck all, and I cannot drop myself in the shit by saying something which is total crap. Life has shown me this: the wise man does not expose himself needlessly to danger.

Well, going through passport control, I did not use my passport; I used my CAC card and hay presto. I got through like the bloody secret service. I got picked up; then I was taken to a hotel about half an hour away. I got my room, went to bed fully exhausted, and woke up at 5 am to the call for prayer. That's what woke me. I thought, fuck me, here again. I went for breakfast, ready for the day to come, where I was going into a war zone. Sometime in the night, the porter posted a letter under the door. Five other people in our group in the hotel, so as I was having my breakfast, I spotted two guys who looked the part. As I went to fill my coffee pot, I just mentioned, "Are you off to Iraq?" One just nodded. So after breakfast, we met at the checkout desk with the others. The guy who nodded said, "Never mention where you or anyone is going. You never know who is listening."

Anyhow, I took that in. We all got in this minibus and went to the airport. We were given an air ticket and a gate number. One or two were coming back off leave, so I tried to ask how it was like in a war zone but did not get much feedback, only that you get mortared and shelled on. We got to the gate for departure and were told there was a delay with the plane. I found out that the plane was a Russian plane, a small Antonov, and the only civilian plane that had the balls to fly in a war zone.

Two hours later, the plane arrived. Fuck me; I could see one of the tires on the plane was down to the wire. I thought this is a fucking death trap. We got on the plane, and it was like being in the Tardis. There was a pilot and co-pilot and an engineer who sat at the back of them and controlled the engines. All of it was manually operated. We took off, no problem. Fifteen minutes later, we were in Iraq, a war zone. We kept flying till we came into Baghdad. Fuck me, from 20,000 feet to landing in 4 minutes so we would not get shot at. We offloaded some people and took off for Kirkuk. The same thing there, down in 4 minutes. We were greeted by some of the team. The plane took off, and we found out later on it would be going to South Africa for some shady deals. Then it would come back a week later. Funny goings-on, I will tell you.

We loaded our gear and headed to the camp, which was a camp inside a camp. We were given keys, told where our rooms were, and to store our gear quickly. After a quick wash, we were told to meet in 1 hour. All I could see were sandbags around the billets and, in the distance, two man-made hills with 2 Oshkosh trucks carrying some sort of radar equipment. But I shall get back to that later.

I got to my room, bare walls, no carpets, just a square box with a fridge, a TV, one table, one chair, and a bed. This was it until my leave in 8 weeks. I got a change of clothes, took a shower, and went back to the main hall. The first thing we did was talk about what happens in a mortar attack, which happens most nights. We were taken around our camp to make sure we knew where the air raid shelters were. Once we found those, we got back to the hall, and our security teams debriefed us on what to do when outside of the wire. We could be shot at by IED or both. This was for real, and I was beginning to like it.

After the debrief, we went into the office. I was shown and met my boss, who said he was an Aussie Brit. He introduced me to our little team and told me where my desk was. He then told me to log in and remember that my computer was being monitored by the USA army, all MI5 stuff. So, I got stuck into the computer, found how to get into our site, made folders, and thought, "What the fuck are we going to be doing?" Not a fucking clue; I had never worked in an office before. I spent the rest of the day smoking, having coffee, and thinking, "What the fuck have I got myself into here?"

Time came and went that day, and we went to the Defacto for tea, that's the Yanks' name for the canteen. Our shift was 11 hours a day, long fucking days in an office. I was going to find out. Went to my room, watched the telly, then went to bed. That night there were no mortars or rockets coming in. I was in bed by 9.

The next morning, I was up and down at the de fact for 6 am. We started work at 7 am. In these defact (canteens), you could have anything you wanted. I went for breakfast - steaks and eggs with a big mug of coffee and 3 rounds of toast. The Yanks used to come in with their rifles, we're just dropped on the floor. No one gave a fuck. They were getting psyched up to go off the wire for the day. My time will come sooner than later.

So, I strolled back to the office around where all the main battle tanks were stored. It always amazed me. There was a time when I met a soldier whose job was to service the tanks. He told me that on many occasions when the tanks came back, there were body parts stuck in the tracks. We just hosed them down the grid.

I got back to the office. It was rocking and rolling. A meeting was arranged for our team, who was on the mechanical side of the job. We, in total, were 15. We all introduced ourselves and said a little bit about ourselves. I said I was a mechanical engineer who had worked in Saudi Arabia, Syria, etc. It went down well. So, we were all given various projects. My first job was the refurbishment of the fire equipment on an oil-filling platform down outside Umm Kasur, around 10 miles out at sea. This was blown up in the Iraq-Iran war years before. Below is an outline of the platform when I was working on it.

Refurbishment Under Coalition Forces

The ABOT platform was refurbished and upgraded under contract W9126G-04-D-0002, with an indefinite delivery, indefinite quantity (IDIQ), and cost-plus award fee with an estimated not-to-exceed value of US$800 million. The contract was between the U.S. Army Corps of Engineers (USACE) of Fort Worth, TX and Parsons Iraqi Joint Venture (PIJV) Houston, TX.

ABOT's capacity was more than doubled to offload up to 3 Mbbl (480,000 m3) of oil per day. Practical constraints in the upstream refinery and oil fields limit actual delivery below the designed maximum.

The dilapidated and fragile nature of the terminal was featured in an NPR story on June 20, 2009, and again on October 4, 2010. Engineers interviewed said that "they didn't even know just how bad the condition of the pipeline is; they didn't dare, despite the work conducted, run it at full pressure for fear it would burst, and they didn't dare shut down the flow to fix it for fear that the weight of the ocean would implode it"; the most recent capacity tests were conducted nearly two decades earlier in 1991.

I was one of those people who were asked the question. I was now big time over 30 years. I had waited for a job like this, as I said earlier to you, if you wait at a barber's shop one day you will get a haircut.

So, that is an outline of the terminal. And as I said, my job was to renew all firefighting equipment. The only thing I had were pictures of the many foam cannons, water cannons, and all pipe work and flanges, nuts, bolts, etc. It was a real tester for me who, in the real world, was not a mechanical engineer, but I was going to give it my best shot and have the balls to think only from week to week. And really, all they can do to me is send me back home to my wife and kids. No more or less. At worst, I could be out of the wire and get blown up. But then my wife would be looked after all her life. One thing the Yanks are good at, remember. People my age then were going home at night, watching the soaps, and being nagged by their wives and kids. Me, I was living my dream with lads with big toys.

Getting back to reality, I was now on my computer. I had gotten around it and made folders, etc. There seemed to be no rush in the office. This, I found out, was because we were all being paid big bucks, so why rush? But that's not me. I wanted to finish this job and run a little project of my own, which later down the line, I did with a very competent engineer who did have a degree. But we gelled because he could do things I had no clue about and the same about me. But that's another 4 months later.

The first of many drop blocks I did in Kirkuk. This was a classic. I asked how to fill in my timesheet, which had to go to top brass for signing every week. I asked this guy who was not on our team but was a Brit. He said, "You do this and that," and he showed me on his computer how he did his. So, I went back to my desk, got it up on my PC, filled it up, and then it said send and print. Underneath, something similar. never thought nothing about it when I got a phone call, so without looking, I picked up the phone and clicked the print button.

Had the conversation on the phone. This was, I had to go on a course on how to fill in forms and documents which are legal documents. I thought this was going to be harder than I thought, so forgetting about my timesheet, I went into another office where there were inspectors who would check your purchases and see if they were correct in a court of law. This took all morning and a bit of the afternoon. All these forms were on my computer, but I sorted the ones I would be using on my screen.

Then this lad who I had never seen before said, "Are you Peter Oldham?" I said, "Yes, that's me." He then said, "Come with me around the other side of the office to the printer." When I arrived, there were reams and reams of paper on the floor. "I have been waiting for this printer since this morning; this shit is yours," he said. "Fuck me," I thought, "what the fuck have I done?" I looked at a few, and they were people's time sheets from all around the Middle East. "Fuck me," I said. "Leave it to me, I will shift it."

Well, it was time to go for the evening meal, so I waited till that part of the office was emptied of people. I found 2 empty filing cabinets and shoved them in there, and started to shred them. This took over a month. I thought that no one else knew about this dropbolock, but 2 years later, I found out that everyone in the office knew but kept it to themselves till I was out of earshot.

First of many dropbolocks, but this job was a cash cow. "Fuck 'em, be the grey man, say fuck all so you cannot drop yourself in it."

THOSE WHO FLY ALONE HAVE THE STRONGEST WINGS

So that was my baptism of fire in the office. I started to smoke again after 10 years. I would go outside and smoke 2 cigs to get my mind on the job, which now was taking its toll. You get nowt for nowt. I kept thinking another week gone, 5 to go before R.R. Every week; I used to do this. Every week, as I said before, this was a cash cow. Keep cool and do your job. They were testing me to see if I had balls and could do the job in question. I was sending out e-mails to all the offshore firefighting companies in ENGLAND for jobs for the lads back home. Once I received them, I had this live folder in which I put all the details, and it told you which company to buy from. Very high-tech. After 2 weeks, they gave me 2 monitors. This is it; they are jellying to me.

Most nights, we got an air raid, either mortars coming in or rockets. We got up, put on our helmets and flak jackets, and made our way to the air raid shelters. Sometimes we got flares going up and artillery firing back at the bad guys. They did this with two trucks loaded with electronic equipment. Both were on a man-made hill, one on one and the other on the other. When they found a missile coming in, they got together and sent the coordinates to the guns. If they fired from a village, the guns never fired back, but in open ground, there would be a barrage of fire from the howitzers. All good fun. I really liked it. At this time, there were teams going out to the oilfields with their security teams. This is what I wanted. Not to be REMF (a rear esalon mother fucker), but it was about to become sooner than later. I now had been there over 8 weeks, been home, come back, and had money in the bank.

One of these was a man who was top of his game in security out there he was ex SAS, I was in his team. There were millions made by a lot of people. One of these was a man who was top of his game in security. Our team is out there, ex-SAS. I got on well with him until an incident happened 18 months later, but after that, we became good friends. That will come later.

So, on my 15th week or so, I was introduced to a young guy who was camp boss on the Euphrates river. The engineers were putting back 3 pipelines on the bottom of the river which were blown up by the Yanks when they came through. On this site was a camp, and this young lad ran it. He was saying they have problems with their water supply and the pumps. I said I would go and fix them; that was my trade (a lie). So, then he said we get shot at and mortared on most days, not a great place to be. And to get there, we have had 2 teams EID (blown up). I said, no prob, get me out of this bullpen for a bit. So, true to his word, he got me out there for a 2-week tour and fixed the pumps.

A few days later, the camp boss and I had a meeting with our security team and coordinator about getting to this remote camp by the river. They said on our way, the bad guys are getting cocky, and we may get some small firearms. They told us of an incident with another team and another company on that road who got ambushed. What you do, you don't stop; you go straight through the firefight. But these lads, one of the last trucks, got hit. The rest bugged out and stopped about a mile down the road. They had a Chinese parliament and decided to go back for the rest of the team and not wait for the army to arrive. They went back, shot the lot of them, had a firefight for half an hour, and rescued the rest of the team before the army came.

I thought, "fucking hell, this is for real now." And, bugger me, the last hour of work that day, the comms office said, "We have a team coming in, not our lads, but this is the nearest camp that's been hit, and one man is seriously hurt." No more than 10 minutes later, three cars came in, full of shrapnel, and one lad who was in the back had been scalped. He did not have his hard hat on, and a piece of shrapnel came through the window and took a piece of skin from the back of his head to the front. What a fucking mess! Blood covered the back of the car. They then drove into the main camp to the army's hospital. The next thing we knew, they could only do so much for him. He was going to be flown to Germany for special treatment. I always think sometimes, "Did he make it?" Life's a funny thing sometimes, but now I am in the big league.

Kirkuk Airbase is located in northern Iraq, approximately 240 kilometers north of Baghdad, on the west side of the city of Kirkuk. It is located 1.6 km west of Kirkuk. The airfield is served by 2 main runways measuring 9,700 and 8,400 feet. It had one 2,800-meter asphalt and one 2,325-meter graded earth runway and one 2,900 m runway under construction by 1991. According to the "Gulf War Air Power Survey," Kirkuk Air Base had 24 hardened aircraft shelters. At each end of the main runway were hardened aircraft shelters known as "trapezoids" or "Yugos," which were built by Yugoslavian contractors some time prior to 1985. Kirkuk Airbase occupied a 9-square-kilometer site and was protected by 12 kilometers of security perimeter.

Prior to 2003, the facility was a major Iraqi Air Force base with support facilities for at least 2 fighter squadrons. It was strategically located near the Kirkuk oil fields and the Kirkuk refinery and petrochemical plant. Kirkuk Air Base was said to be home to a Sector Operations Centre and an Intercept Operations Centre.

After the US invasion in 2003, the facility became home to a US Air Force airbase (referred to informally at least initially as "Krab town") and Army logistical hub (FOB Warrior). As of April 2005, there were about 1,000 U.S. Air Force and 2,500 Army personnel stationed at Kirkuk. Another 1,500 people, mostly non-Iraqis, were employed at the base.

War is what happens when language fails.

Well, after a couple of days, they got a team together to take me to the river camp which was on the other side of the river. We got across by landing craft (don't ask how that got there). So the day came; I got my rucksack with enough clothes for 3 days and had an informal meeting with the security team. They did say it was getting worse on the road down there, so don't panic; you are in good hands. It was a real eye-opener for me. I am now going out of the wire, and I may not come back. Fucking hell, I really did not think of death. My problem was I might go blind over the 2 years out there. That was the only thing I did not worry about losing a limb or two, but going blind was the one for me. So the security team saddled up, and the last two in were me and head shed of the convoy. We radioed in to the USA army, got a slot time 24 hours ago, still had the slot time, and off we fucking went. First 10 miles, I was told there will be no problem.

But after that, we shall be in an Indian country. All the teams on this patrol were Brits, ex-Marines, and ex-Paras. If we were going to get some shit, I was with the best. I remembered our drills for changing cars if EID, which we practiced once a month. Now one hour down the road, no problem. But then, on a side road, we saw three cars keeping abreast to us. So quickly, we turned into the desert, and we lost them. That was it for me on this trip. We got back on track and we came to an outer circle of Iraqis, all tooled up. The Yanks had paid them to watch this camp's outer limits 24 hours a day. We came speeding down to the river. This 2nd World War landing craft was waiting for me. I got out and was taken down to the front of the boat, and was given to the lads on the boat for security. The lads took some paperwork, etc., from the camp, and they then headed back to Kirkuk Airbase. Before dusk fell, you did not want to be traveling in the dark out there. I got on board and met this Yorkshire man who, over the 2 years I got pally with. He told me about the camp and the mortar attacks most nights. I got to the other side, and the camp boss was waiting for me. I got in his truck, and we drove to the camp about 1000 yards away. As I was looking back over the river, I could see that they were welding some 40-inch oil pipes to go across the river. These lads used to get morted on around twice a week. So, I was shown to my bedroom. It was covered outside with sandbags. I was told the day was fucked now. "I will show you the pumps that you want to look at tomorrow. Have some scran; then we shall have a drink." Fuck me, general order number one. We were on no booze, no fraternizing with the opposite sex, etc., etc.

Now, I had an evening meal and got introduced to many who worked out there full-time. I got to feel I was a team player, not someone they wanted to catch out with. So, after the evening meal, I found the camp boss's hooch. Went inside; it was wall-to-wall booze, so there were a few of us having a drink. By 8 o'clock, I was pissed.

They had given me a strong lager, so I thought time to go. I just about found my hooch. I crashed out, dead to the world, till I heard sirens, heavy thuds, and people shouting. Fuck me; we are under attack! Could I find my flak vest? The helmet was under the bed. By the time I got out and found the air raid shelter, I was the last in and smelling of booze. The head shed of security smelt my breath and said we shall have a word in the morning. The mortars coming in lasted about 20 minutes, then the all-clear went off. I got back to my hooch, wide awake and bushy-tailed. I thought fucking great, this shit. So, I did get back off and, around 7 am, woke up, had a shower, then went for breakfast. After that, the head shed came and found me, gave me a fucking bollocking about being pissed, and we were all on general order number one. We work for the American army, don't forget. After the bollocking, we introduced each other, and to be fair, he turned out to be a good scout over the coming years.

So, I was taken to the workshop, found some tools, and made my way to the pumping station. Straight away, I found the problem. The generators, which gave power to the pump, were not running well. All the filters were blocked with sand. Why no one ever knew this is beyond me. They all wanted to be desk jockeys, but my background was on tools. So, I thought I would play them at their own game. I liked it here, so I shall write my first report that it will take 4 days to sort out, plus I will sort any other shit that needed doing to keep the camp working.

I sent an email to the main office head shed in Kirkuk, and his reply was to stay until the job was completed. This now gave me free rein of the camp and river crossing. Happy days! I used to have a good breakfast, a light lunch, and a big tea, and then always someone said, "Come to my place for a drink." But after four days of drinking and waking up to the sirens and going to the bunkers, I was getting fed up. So, I spent the last three nights in my hooch with food from the canteen, watching films and DVDs. I was in my element. I was booked to go back to Kirkuk in three days. I could have spent more time there, but intel said the bad guys were getting stronger by the day. "You will be the last to go by road. After you, we shall chopper men in. Plus, we have a mortar team flying in tomorrow to give the insurgents something back," they said.

So, the next day, the mortar team flew in and set up two mortars, the biggest fuckers I have ever seen. So, come the night, we got incoming, and then the mortar team let rip. They must have sent at least 20 over to them. How they knew where they were was a mystery to me, but I found out they had an OAP out in the field giving coordinates. By the time I left, there was no more incoming, but I found out much later that when the mortar team left, the bad guys started all over again.

When it was my time to leave the FOB (Forward Operating Base), I went out with another lad who was going on RR. We were the last to go by road for a very long time. The day after, everything was chopped in, as was the personnel.

Before we left, we waited for the landing craft to come from the other side. The front opened and a shout of "Number one, you going now!" It was the lad who took me to the camp from the other side of the river. Our paths would meet again in Basra. When we got to the other side, and the ramp went down, I could imagine what it must have been like on D-day. My team picked me up and took me to the convoy. The other guy and I were classified as the package. We received intel on what we might expect and were told to keep an eye out for the bad guys. However, as it happened, we only got a few stray shots fired at us, so the drive back to Kirkuk was really a normal day in Iraq.

I got back to base, and it was time to call it a day. The next day, I did my report on what I had done and sent it off. It was about this time I was getting a bit of shit about my reports. I was using spell check, but some words were not right at all. I realized I am dyslexic. I have had it since I was a boy, and no one picked it up, only the USA Army. Good skills to them.

The purpose of our lives is to be happy." — Dalai Lama.

Well, got my feet under the table again at base camp, but I wanted to be going out of the wire more. I was loving it - big kids with big toys. So, I asked my boss about giving me something out of the wire. His reply was, "if we do, you will not get any more money," but I was on enough anyhow. The following day, he said there was a big project coming up in Basra which is up my street - taking out 25 large pumps and taking them to Dubai for a strip down and refurb. That in itself is a nightmare - remember, we are in a war zone. You cannot just take something out of the country. You need armed convoys. I said yes, put me down for it. Then he said, "your boss on the mechanical side is Mr. Moody, Senior Engineer." He is a bit of an eccentric, but you shall both get on, I can tell. What that meant, I do not know but I was about to find out. He told me, "once you have finished ordering for ABOT (the firefighting equipment), you can join the team who are in the other building." I thought, yes, I must be doing good to get a shot at it. It took me a week to finish the job in question.

So, on a Sunday morning, I was introduced to Mr. Moody. He was a Texan with a proper drawl in his talk. We got introduced, and I spent a full day with him. He was getting to know me, and the same about him. This was really an informal interview. I knew this, so I became the grey man - not bullshitting because I did not know if he was any good or not, but we seemed to hit it off. The next day, he introduced me to the team - 2 electricians (high voltage), 2 civils, and 2 instrument technicians. They all seemed a good bunch. Well, we must all be mad to be here in the first place. All people our age were taking their grandkids out and taking them to school. We were in a fucking war zone for the USA COR OF ENGINEERS, on General Order Number One, which months down the line will bite me in the arse.

So, the next day, I packed my shit away and moved into our building, which was full of Texan and American flags. The group was all Texans - the one-star state. I was the only Brit on the team. I was shown to my desk - 2 computers. I had never had 2 computers side by side. Did not ask why but found out later in the week by watching the others. They think I am a Mechanical Engineer with a fucking degree.

After a couple of days, I was slowly getting into the swing of things. Mr moody was telling me what I should be doing and what documents to fill in after one week at Kirkuck. I was told we should be going to Basra next week. We have digs and an office to work from, and a security team will be with us to take us out of the wire. I could not wait to bring it on.

When you get tired, learn to rest.

So the big day came to leave Kirkuk. I was ready to leave. I was not a big player, just a number in Kirkuk, but this would change our security teams that were already in place down in Basra.

Let's start with why I wrote this book. My rationale was simple. I wrote it to fill a void. It is a sad fact that much of the debate over private military and security contractors is, to borrow from Shakespeare, a tale told by idiots, full of sound and fury, signifying nothing. The tale is made worse by the fact that many of those doing the telling have highly partisan axes to grind.

I have been following the industry since the early 1990s, long before I moved into Iraq, even realizing there was a PMC sector. As time passed, it became clear that an interesting, indeed fairly important subject, the role and impact of outsourcing the traditional military and other national security functions, was degenerating into a politicized debate.

This book is simply a modest attempt to bring some facts into view and let the chips fall where they may. In general, there has been far too much sensationalistic, sometimes misleading coverage of how and why tasks formerly done in-house by the U.S. military have been outsourced, especially in regard to Iraq. Now that PMCs are becoming embedded in popular culture via film, popular books, cartoons, and television, the time is long overdue for a factual, dispassionate accounting of both the good and bad of the subject.

Let's be honest about this. The fact that we are dealing with an industry that has really only been in the public eye for a bit over a decade, depending on who and where you count, makes drawing conclusions difficult. Quite simply, it is, despite notable consolidations in recent years, an industry in flux. Ten years ago, most public commentaries focused on just three companies, Executive Outcomes and Sandline of Great Britain (both of which no longer exist) and U.S.-based MPRI (now a subsidiary of L 3).

A quick note on terminology is in order. In this book, I write about private security contractors (PSCs). These are firms that employ people who carry weapons to protect their clients and use them when necessary. Such firms are often labeled "private military contractors," although that more accurately refers to firms doing unarmed logistics work, such as KBR.

PSCs are generally considered a subset of PMCs. Academics have spent years arguing over the appropriate terminology. I largely consider it an academic distinction that doesn't have much relevance to the real-world discussion of the subject. But for the sake of convenience-because, the acronym is already firmly embedded in popular culture, and discourse-I generally use PMC, although I am writing specifically about PSCs, an acronym I use as well.

There is no consensus on what constitutes a PMC, but three main categories of their activities stand out:

• *Military combatant companies* - Firms that actually provide military forces capable of combat are fairly rare and only constitute a minority of PMCs, even though such firms tend to receive the most publicity. Examples include the now-disbanded PMCs Executive Outcomes of South Africa and Sandline of the United Kingdom; none are currently operating in Iraq.

- ***Military consulting firms*** - These traditionally provide training and advisory services, though some have expanded into personal security and bodyguard services. Examples include Blackwater, MPRI, DynCorp, and SAIC of the United States.

- ***Military support firms*** - These provide non-lethal aid and assistance, such as weapons maintenance, technical support, explosive ordnance disposal, and intelligence collection and analysis. Examples include Halo Group, Vinnell, and Ronco of the United States.

Put aside, for a moment, the reality that as nations have frayed, private security contractors are far from the only type of group that has taken a bite out of the monopoly of violence traditionally assumed by states. Think of gangs in urban ghettos or factions in failed states, for example. The truth is that defining a mercenary is a bit like defining pornography; it is frequently in the eye and mind of the beholder. From the viewpoints of accountability or regulation, words that have been cited innumerable times over the past few years in regard to private security contractors, the only definition that counts is the legal one.

The most widely, if not universally accepted, definition is that in the 1977 Protocol I to the Geneva Conventions. Article 47 puts forward six criteria, all of which must be met for a combatant to be considered a mercenary. Accordingly, a mercenary is any person who:

a. Is specially recruited locally or abroad in order to fight in an armed conflict;

b. Does, in fact, take a direct part in the hostilities;

c. Is motivated to take part in the hostilities essentially by the desire for private gain and, in fact, is promised, by or on behalf of a Party to the conflict, material compensation substantially in excess of that promised or paid to combatants of similar ranks and functions in the armed forces of that Party;

d. Is neither a national of a Party to the conflict nor a resident of territory controlled by a Party to the conflict;

e. Is not a member of the armed forces of a Party to the conflict; and

f. Has not been sent by a State that is not a Party to the conflict on official duty as a member of its armed forces.

So why wouldn't someone working for a private security contractor in Iraq, for example, meet that definition? Well, for starters, a majority of those working for private security contractors are Iraqi, and as such, are nationals of a party to the conflict, so they don't qualify. Second, not all private security workers take a direct part in the hostilities.

There are at least 200 foreign and domestic private security companies in Iraq, ranging from major firms such as Aegis Defence Services, ArmorGroup, Blackwater USA Group, DynCorp, and Triple Canopy to far smaller ones. Not all their employees are out there toting guns. Some of their consultancy services are extremely white-collar, involving work such as sitting in front of computer consoles at Regional Operations Centres and monitoring convoy movements.

Some people consider PMCs (or PSCs) simply patriotic Americans willing to do their part in supporting America, just like regular military forces. But others consider them thinly veiled mercenaries. Typical is this view by Yale English professor David Bromwich:

"A far more consequential euphemism, in the conduct of the Iraq war, and a usage adopted without demur until recently by journalists, lawmakers, and army officers, speaks of mercenary soldiers as contractors or security (the last now a singular-plural like the basketball teams called Magic and Jazz). The Blackwater killings in Baghdad's Nissour Square on September 16, 2007, brought this euphemism, and the extraordinary innovation it hides, suddenly to public view. Yet the armed Blackwater guards who did the shooting, though now less often described as mere 'contractors,' are referred to as employees, a neutral designation that repels further attention. The point about mercenaries is that you employ them when your army is inadequate to the job assigned. This has been the case from the start in Iraq."

But the fact that the mercenaries have been continuously augmented until they now outnumber American troops suggests a truth about the war that falls open to inspection only when we use the accurate word. It was always known to the Office of the Vice President and the Department of Defense that the conventional forces they deployed were smaller than would be required to maintain order in Iraq. That is why they hired the extracurricular forces.

Putting aside the fact that historically speaking, a mercenary hasn't always been a dirty word, the truth is more complex. There are both good and bad aspects to private military contracting, and I've mentioned both in past writings. Admittedly, the line between the two is often hard to discern. One British commentator noted:

"When I asked an official at the Foreign Office a question about mercenaries last week, he replied, 'they're not mercenaries; they're private security companies.' 'What's the difference?' 'The difference is that a private security company is a properly registered company, not an individual getting a few friends together.' In other words, you cease to be a mercenary by sending £20 to Companies House."

And it is true that there are connections between the worlds of classic mercenaries and security contractors.

For example, consider Simon Mann, a former British Army officer, a South African citizen, and a mercenary. In 2004, he was accused of planning to overthrow the government of oil-rich Equatorial Guinea. His coup attempt was viewed as a real-life version of the 1974 novel The Dogs of War by Frederick Forsyth, which chronicled the efforts of a company of European mercenary soldiers hired by a British industrialist to depose the government of a fictional African country.

Interestingly, in recent years, after the release of once-secret British government documents, Forsyth was forced to admit his own role in financing a similar, and similarly failed, a coup against Equatorial Guinea in 1973. Mann is a former associate of Lieutenant Colonel Tim Spicer, the chief executive of the British private military contractor Aegis Defence-one of the biggest security firms currently in Iraq-having worked with him in another private security firm, Sandline International. Forsyth was an investor when Spicer first set up Aegis, and he reportedly made quite a big wedge of money from his investment.

But Mann also helped establish Executive Outcomes. That firm was the mother of all private security contractors and the missing link between the "Wild Geese"-style mercenaries of old and the new generation of PMCs. Executive Outcomes was renowned around the world in the 1990s for fighting against rebel leader Jonas Savimbi in Angola and against the murderous Revolutionary United Front rebel group in Sierra Leone.

Nowadays, people tend to label anyone who carries a gun while not a member of a regular military establishment a mercenary. Such people are supposedly uncontrollable rogues who commit unspeakable atrocities and wreak havoc. As a member of an industry trade group put it, "The term 'mercenary' is commonly used to describe the private peace and stability operations industry by opponents and those who lack a fundamental understanding of exactly what it is that the industry does. Regardless, it is a popular pejorative term among those who don't particularly care for the private sector's role in peace and stability operations."

Well, war is war, and violence is an inextricable part of it. But even the worst of classical mercenaries from ancient times or the Middle Ages would have a hard time rivaling the record of human and physical destruction achieved by regular military forces. For example, mercenaries did not invent concentration camps, firebomb cities from the air, use chemical or biological weapons or use nuclear weapons on civilian cities. In fact, the bloodiest century in recorded human history was the twentieth, courtesy of regular military forces. Not even the most bloodthirsty mercenaries of centuries past could have imagined committing the kind of carnage for which contemporary regular military forces routinely plan and train.

And, just to confuse things a little more, one might note that there are tens of thousands of people serving in the American military who aren't even American, at least not yet. The number increased from 28,000 to 39,000 from 2000 to 2005 alone. Many of them applied under a fast-track process approved by President Bush in 2003 and enacted in October 2004. Under the new rules, people in the military can become citizens without paying the customary $320 application fee or having to be in the United States for an interview with immigration officials and naturalization proceedings. The President also made thousands of service members immediately eligible for citizenship by not requiring them to meet a minimum residency threshold, as civilians applying to be citizens must do, although they must still be legal residents of the United States.

In late 2006, it was reported that the U.S. military, struggling to meet recruiting goals, was considering opening up recruiting stations overseas and putting more immigrants on a faster track to U.S. citizenship if they volunteered. Such proposals have been catching on among parts of the establishment. Michael O'Hanlon, a senior fellow at the Brookings Institution in Washington, and Max Boot, a senior fellow at the Council on Foreign Relations in New York, have proposed allowing thousands of immigrants into the United States to serve for four years in the military in exchange for citizenship.

In any event, such immigrants are fighting, and in some cases dying, for a country of which they are not a part, but we don't call them mercenaries. As of March 2008, more than 100 foreign-born members of the U.S. military had earned American citizenship by dying in Iraq.

In fact, in the current age, in which modern state militaries are staffed by volunteer recruits largely joining in peacetime—many for the pay and benefits—the difference between the private and public soldiers appears to revolve largely around the form of employment contract.

I believe there is another side to the use of private security and military contractors that few people care to talk about publicly. The reality is that private contractors did not crawl out from under a rock somewhere. They are on America's battlefields because the government, reflecting the will of the people, wants them there.

The reason we have such reliance on private contractors is simple enough. Even though the Cold War is over and the Soviet Union is a historical memory, the United States still reserves the right to militarily intervene everywhere. This, however, despite the so-called Revolution in Military Affairs that Defense Secretary Donald Rumsfeld championed, is a highly people-powered endeavor. And most people have decided that their children, much like Dick Cheney during the Vietnam War, have "better things to do."

Looking at it historically, however, it wasn't supposed to be this way. As one scholar noted:

"When the U.S. military shifted to an all-volunteer professional force in the wake of the Vietnam War, military leaders set up a series of organization 'trip wires' to preserve the tie between the nation's foreign policy decisions and American communities. Led by then Army Chief of Staff Gen. Creighton Abrams (1972–74), they wanted to ensure that the military would not go to war without the sufficient backing and involvement of the nation. But much like a corporate call center moved to India, this 'Abrams Doctrine' has since been outsourced."

But, given the downsizing the U.S. armed forces had undergone since the fall of the Berlin Wall, the military turned to the private sector for help.

My own view of the world is that the international order will continue to be roiled and disrupted for some time to come. Thus, there will be a void in international politics. And, just as in nature, which abhors a vacuum, private contractors will step in to fill it. Personally, I think the outsourcing of military capabilities left the station decades ago. It has taken this long for public perception to catch up - and people still only see the caboose.

If people don't want to use private contractors, the choices are simple. Either scale back U.S. geopolitical commitments or enlarge the military, something that will entail more gargantuan expenditures and even, some argue, a return to the draft down the road.

Personally, I prefer the former. But most people prefer substituting contractors for draftees. As former Marine colonel Jack Holly said, "We're never going to war without the private security industry again in a non-draft environment."

Still, what I would really like to see is a national debate on this. Instead, we bury our heads in the sand and bemoan the presence of private contractors. That is a waste of time. Private security contractors, after all, are just doing the job we outsourced to them. And, like them or hate them, they are going to be around for a long time.

As Paul Lombardi, CEO of DynCorp, said in 2003, "You could fight without us, but it would be difficult. Because we're so involved, it's difficult to extricate us from the process." And as Professor Debra Avant noted, "A lot of the companies in the 1990s were small, service-based companies. Now they're small services-based wings of large companies. Defense contractors have been buying up these companies like mad. This is where they think the future is."

Permit a brief overview. As Shakespeare wrote, "Cry "Havoc!" and let slip the dogs of war. But the question is, whose dogs exactly?

Traditionally, the ultimate symbol of the sovereignty of a nation is its ability to monopolize the means of violence - in other words, raising, maintaining, and using military forces. Although there have always been exceptions, such as partisans and guerrilla forces, the evolution of the international system over the centuries has been such that military conflict has been conducted using state-raised forces. Of course, even during that evolution, private contractors played significant roles. Some of the same criticisms made against private contractors today were made against the East India Company back in the 17th to 19th centuries. Indeed, it was the East India Company that pioneered the shareholder model of corporate ownership.

In modern times these forces have been motivated by issues of nationalism and ideology in opposition to earlier traditions of fighting for whoever could pay. The evolution of national military establishments has also been accompanied by changes in international law that, though often belatedly and imperfectly, seek to regulate the means by which military force is used, including the types of military units considered legitimate.

According to estimates from the International Peace Operations Association, the global "Peace and Stability Operations Industry" total industry value is $20 billion for all companies providing services in the field. Of that number, private security contractors (PSCs) make up only about 5 to 10 percent of the total (approximately $2 billion annually of total industry value). Although the normal peacetime number would be closer to 5 percent for PSCs, events in Iraq have driven the number up.

But the industry is seen as a growth sector. In September 2005, the Stockholm International Peace Research Institute said that the industry was likely to double in size over the next five years, confirming predictions that industry revenues would hit $200 billion in 2010.

The military's growing reliance on contractors is part of a government-wide shift toward outsourcing that goes back decades. During the Clinton administration, it was promoted as "Reinventing Government" by former Vice President Al Gore, an initiative that promised that cutting government payrolls and shifting work to contractors would improve productivity while cutting costs. In early 2005, the federal government was spending about $100 billion more annually on outside contracts than on employee salaries. Many federal departments and offices-NASA and the Department of Energy, to name just two-have become de facto contract management agencies, devoting upward of 80 percent of their budgets to contractors.

Not to be outdone, in 2000, presidential candidate George W. Bush promised to let private companies compete with government workers for 450,000 jobs. As recently as 2003, Defense Secretary Donald Rumsfeld said that as many as 320,000 jobs filled by military personnel could be turned over to civilians. By even the narrowest interpretation, the PMC sector dates back at least 15 years, to when the then-little-known South African firm, Executive Outcomes, started gaining world attention for its operations against Jonas Savimbi's UNITA in Angola. But there has certainly been a recent expansion.

In the United States, one can trace the push for the outsourcing of military activities back to the 1966 release of the revised Office of Management and Budget (OMB) Circular A-76.51. Private contractors were prominent in the "nation-building" effort in South Vietnam and grew significantly over the decades that followed. Certainly, the use of private contractors by the U.S. military has been an increasing trend.

In the United States, the PMC industry was fueled by the same zeal for the market-based approaches that drove the deregulation of the electricity, airline, and telephone-service industries. The military was considered to be particularly well-suited to public-private partnerships because the need for its services fluctuates so radically and abruptly. In light of such sharp spikes in demand, it was thought it would be more efficient for the military to call on a group of temporary, highly trained experts in times of war, even if that meant paying them a premium rather than relying on a permanent standing army that drained resources (with pension plans, health insurance, and so forth) in times of peace.

Now it should be noted that the jury is still out, in terms of hard evidence, whether the facts support the ideology.

One article noted:

[Outsourcing support functions is] a tidy picture: the Army becomes a lean, mean killing machine, while civilians peel the potatoes and clean the latrines. But there's a reason that companies like General Motors existed in the first place. Effective as outsourcing can be, doing things in-house is often easier and quicker. You avoid the expense and hassle of haggling and retain operational reliability and control, which is especially important to the military. No contract can guarantee that private employees will stick around in a combat zone. After the Iraq war, some contractors refused assignments to dangerous parts of the country. That left American troops sitting in the mud and without hot food…

Outsourcing works well when there's genuine competition among suppliers; that's when the virtues of the private sector come into play. But in the market for big military contracts, the bidders tend to be the usual few suspects, so the game resembles the American auto or steel industries before Japan and Germany became major players: more comfortable than competitive. Sometimes the lack of competition is explicit: many of the contracts for rebuilding Iraq were handed out on a no-bid basis. And many of them are "cost-plus" contracts. This means that the contractors' profit is a percentage of their costs, which gives them the incentive to keep those costs high. That's hardly a recipe for efficiency or rigor.

In the past, Blackwater itself, the 800-pound gorilla of private security contractors, acknowledged that the cost-benefit claim is still undecided. This was seen in October 2, 2007, hearing of the U.S. House Oversight and Government Reform Committee at which Erik Prince, the founder and head of Blackwater, testified. Mr. Prince was asked about the cost-benefit of using private contractors:

Mr. Prince said, "I don't know what those numbers are, sir, but that would be a great fully burden cost study that Congress could sponsor. They don't have to do the whole thing, just take some key nodes and really study it."

An economic professor wrote, "The use of private contractors erodes checks and balances, and it substitutes market transactions controlled by the executive branch for traditional political mechanisms of accountability. When it comes to Iraq, we've yet to see the evidence of a large practical gain in return; instead, the use of contractors may have helped to make an ill-advised venture possible."

Many academics who examine the issue of the relative cost of private versus public point to the politics behind the various ways one can measure cost. What you include or exclude in your study can be a complicated political exercise. Economists disagree on how to answer this question, at least in part because they use different variables when measuring cost. When you measure the savings of using retired special operations forces personnel, do you factor in the hundreds of thousands of tax dollars used to train these ex-soldiers? This is a valid economic variable worth including, but no study yet published seems to have done so. Even more difficult can be attaching a dollar value to in-house military 'services.' Because military establishments often have a 'monopoly' of service delivery and information regarding cost, getting accurate comparative information is not easy.

Privatization has been touted as one way to actually allow a government the ability to see cost comparisons between, say, what the army will charge and what a private provider would charge. It is not a bad idea, but problems arise when cost reductions are assumed or when statistics measuring savings from outsourcing are based on hypothetical projections.

Furthermore, 'cost' is not the only way to measure value. Logistics officers often talk about value in terms of cost/speed of delivery/quality of service. If you need it tomorrow in a war zone, you can't expect Federal Express to get it there for you. That affects quality and price. The private and public sectors might-and do-behave differently because of inherent differences between these two sectors.

What little cost-benefit analysis there has been to date has focused on narrow economic cost comparisons and has generally avoided addressing equally important political factors, such as avoiding tough political choices concerning military needs, reserve call-ups, and the human consequences of war.

Nevertheless, the fact that outsourcing military functions from the public to the private sector has not been proven to be more cost-effective and has not stopped people from claiming that it is so. Typical of this is the statement by Doug Brooks, president of the International Peace Operations Association, that are cost-effective. "Although the popular perception is of huge salaries for cushy jobs, the reality is that contractors live alongside military personnel and generally cost the government far less in the long run."

In truth, recent events in Iraq are far from the first time the U.S. government has turned to the private sector for help. Before the 1990s privatization push, private firms had periodically been used in lieu of U.S. forces to enforce covert military policies outside the view of Congress and the public. Examples range from Civil Air Transport and Air America, the CIA's secret paramilitary air arm from 1946 through 1976-prominently used during the Vietnam War-to the use of Southern Air Transport to run guns to Nicaragua in the Iran-Contra scandal.

Historically speaking, in fact, the story goes back even further. Privateers, or private ships licensed to carry out warfare, helped win the American Revolution and the War of 1812. In World War II, the Flying Tigers, American fighter pilots hired by the government of Chiang Kai-Shek, helped defeat the Japanese.

The only point I try to make with these figures is that the use of civilians in American military operations goes back to the founding of the country. Beyond that, any comparisons are problematic because of differences caused by the changes in military control.

For example, none of the eras cited used volunteer armies. Civilian workers in the Revolutionary War were sutlers. These were merchants traveling behind the columns who each night, would sell the troops extra items not supplied by the military (jam for the hardtack, liquor, better shoes, and so on). They were not part of the war effort in the way we talk about today, and they certainly did not provide a personal security detail for General George Washington.

Thus we can say that the private military industry is neither as new nor as big as is frequently claimed. Also, it is evident that civilians have always been instrumental to military operations and have often been in harm's way in support of the military.

So what is new? Specifically, the past two to three decades have seen increased prominence given to the reemergence of an old phenomenon: the existence of organizations working solely for profit. The modern twist, however, is that rather than being ragtag bands of adventurers, paramilitary forces, or individuals recruited clandestinely by governments to work in specific covert operations, the modern firm is solidly corporate. Instead of organizing clandestinely, such firms now operate out of office suites, have public affairs staffs and Web sites, and offer marketing literature.

But although they like to call themselves private security firms, such organizations are clearly quite different from the traditional private security industry that provides watchmen and building security.

Some questions, despite being increasingly asked over the past few years, are still unanswered: How many private security firms work in Iraq? How many contractors do they employ? How many contractors have been wounded or killed? What cost is incurred in such operations?

For the first three years of Operation Iraqi Freedom, the U.S. government had no accurate count of its contractors. As recently as December 2006, the Iraq Study Group estimated that only 5,000 civilian contractors worked in Iraq. The same month, however, Central Command issued the results of its own internal review: about 100,000 government contractors, not counting subcontractors, were operating in Iraq. Then, in February 2007, the Associated Press reported 120,000 contractors working in Iraq.

A Government Accountability Office report released in July 2005 noted that neither the Department of State, the Department of Defense, nor the U.S. Agency for International Development has complete data available on the costs of using PSCs.

In December 2006, the *Washington Post* reported that about 100,000 government contractors were operating in Iraq, not counting subcontractors,-a total approaching the size of the U.S. military force there. That finding, which includes Americans, Iraqis, and third-party nationals hired by companies operating under U.S. government contracts, was significantly higher and wider in scope than the Pentagon's only previous estimate, which claimed that 25,000 security contractors were in the country. It is also 10 times the estimated number of contractors that were deployed during the Persian Gulf War in 1991.

Reporting a major milestone, the *Los Angeles Times* wrote in July 2007 that the number of U.S.-paid private contractors in Iraq exceeded that of American combat troops. More than 180,000 civilians, including Americans, foreigners, and Iraqis, were working in Iraq under U.S. contracts, according to State and Defense Department figures. The numbers include at least 21,000 Americans, 43,000 foreign contractors, and about 118,000 Iraqis. That number, by the way, is still bigger than U.S. military forces, even after the United States increased the number of forces during its 2007 "surge." Furthermore, private security contractors were not fully counted in the survey-so the total contractor number was even larger.

The truth is, for most of the time since the United States went to war in both Afghanistan and Iraq, the Pentagon simply didn't know how many contractors worked in the U.S. Central Command's area of responsibility, which includes both countries.

Some questions, despite being increasingly asked over the past few years, are still unanswered: How many private security firms work in Iraq? How many contractors do they employ? How many contractors have been wounded or killed? What cost is incurred in such operations?

We may be getting closer to answers though. For example, back in February 2007, a relatively unknown senator named Barack Obama introduced the Transparency and Accountability in Military and Security Contracting Act, which required federal agencies to report to Congress the numbers of security contractors, types of military and security equipment used, numbers of contractors killed and wounded, and disciplinary actions taken against contractors.

What kind of casualties do contractors suffer? In February 2006, it was reported that 505 civilian contractors had died in Iraq since the beginning of the war. Another 4,744 contractors have been injured, according to insurance claims on file at the U.S. Department of Labor.

As of December 2006, at least 770 contractors had been killed in Iraq and at least 7,700 wounded. According to U.S. Labor Department statistics, the first three months of 2007 brought the highest number of contract worker deaths for any quarter since the beginning of the

Iraq war. At least 146 contract workers were killed, topping the previous quarterly record of 112 killed at the end of 2004. From August 2004 to the beginning of June 2007, 138 private security workers were killed, and 451 were wounded.

In May 2007, the *New York Times* reported the total number of contractors killed in Iraq to be at least 917, along with more than 12,000 wounded in battle or injured on the job. Those statistics suggested that for every four American soldiers who die in Iraq, a contractor is killed.

By the end of June 2007, the number of contractors killed in Iraq reached 1,001. But these numbers were likely understated, for the data only showed the number of cases reported to the Labor Department, not the total number of injuries or deaths that occurred. The Department broke down 776 contractor deaths by company, leaving out almost a fourth for unspecified reasons, and did not include all companies whose employees or contractors have died in the war.

A report by the U.S. Government Accounting Office in April 2005 found that monitoring of civilian contractors in Iraq was so poor that there was no way to determine how many contractors were working on U.S.-related security and reconstruction projects in Iraq or how many had been killed.

At the end of January 2005, a quarterly report sent to Congress by the inspector general appointed to audit U.S.-funded work in Iraq found that at least 232 civilians had been killed while working on U.S.-funded contracts in Iraq, and the death toll was rising rapidly. It cited U.S. Labor Department statistics showing that companies had filed 232 compensation claims under the Defense Base Act for workers killed there, an increase of 93 percent in the fourth quarter of 2004.

In this sense, outsourcing is advantageous for the administration. For example, it allows the administration to push costs that would otherwise be incurred by Veterans Affairs not just off the books but out of government altogether, at least for now. Although those costs may be hidden in the short term and deferred in the middle term, they will have to be borne eventually. But instead of being addressed in a comprehensive, cost-effective way, the problems will be diffused, and the burdens carried by individual families and communities. Think of the long-term social costs associated with the veterans returning from Vietnam, but without the government and social service available to veterans. Those services have rarely been as generous as Vietnam veterans deserve, but at least we had a framework and means for providing such services.

Some say that contractors, motivated perhaps by profit, deserve less than the troops. But had it not been for contractors, we would have needed more troops. So we would have had to pay the price one way or the other. However, part of the reason for using contract workers in Iraq was to avoid the political ramifications of calling up and paying for the number of troops that were actually needed.

At most, contractors who are killed get an obituary buried in the back pages of their hometown newspaper, based on a press release by their employer or perhaps a brief mention by a government spokesman if the contractor's client was a U.S. government agency.

Numbers like these tend to confirm the view long held by many observers of the industry that one reason government likes to turn to contractors is that it lowers their political costs. Bluntly put: if you are not on active duty in the U.S. military-even if you were for 10 to 20 years previously-and even if you are contributing to the war effort, nobody beyond your immediately family cares if you get killed.

Who works for these firms? PMCs are employing personnel from numerous countries around the world, not only the United States. Contractors come from Bosnia, Britain, Nepal, Chile, Ukraine, Israel, South Africa, New Zealand, Australia, and Fiji, not to mention those who served in the French Foreign Legion, to name just some countries. It is globalization in action. Though they are doing a wide variety of tasks in Iraq, the common link is helping, in one way or another, to provide security. Personnel from one country who is recruited by a company in another country to work in yet another country are called third-country nationals (TCNs). The Pentagon says that 30 percent of contract personnel in Iraq are so-called TCNs.

Let's turn to oversight for a moment. It is simply inarguable that proper monitoring of contracts was woefully deficient in the first few years of the U.S. occupation of Iraq. And it still leaves much to be desired. A Government Accountability Office report released in March 2008 said that the Pentagon relies too much on contractors who often work alongside their government counterparts, cost more, and sometimes take on responsibilities they are not supposed to. The report said that as the government's workforce has shrunk, its demand for services has mushroomed, and procurement deals have become more complex and hard to manage. That has forced agencies to hire more contractors. In 2007 the Defense Department spent $158.3 billion on services, a 76 percent increase over the past decade and more than what it spends on supplies, equipment, and major weapons systems.

The GAO looked at the Army Contracting Agency's Contracting Center of Excellence (CCE), which does procurement for 125 divisions at the Pentagon. It found that 42 percent of the Army's CCE procurement specialists are contractors, up from 24 percent in fiscal 2005. The report said that relying so much on contractors creates "the risk of loss of government control over and accountability" for government programs.

Some companies early on argued that greater care should be taken in vetting the qualifications of their employees. Back in September 2004, Armour Group, the London-based company, published a white paper arguing that companies offering armed guards abroad should be vetted under the 2001 Private Security Industry Act. At that time, only companies offering services within the United Kingdom were covered by the law.

Christopher Beese, director of ArmorGroup International, said, "It seems extraordinary that the doorman for a nightclub, catering for a particular clientele in a particular part of town, may have to be vetted and licensed when the same man can be equipped with a rifle and an armored vehicle and be engaged to protect diamond concessions for a foreign regime in clear breach of public interest and perhaps even in contravention of human rights, but needs no such regulation."

About six months later, a spokesman for ArmorGroup said: "We are demanding regulation. It is extraordinary that door supervisors have to be licensed, but any Joe Public can get a Kalashnikov and work with a security company abroad. This is an issue of accountability, as these companies can be set up so quickly."

Of course, what constitutes proper vetting is debatable. In March 2006, five years after Mr. Beese's statement, British Foreign Secretary Jack Straw said that armed U.K. security guards working in Iraq could be checked by the Security Industry Authority, the same body that vets British pub bouncers.

ArmorGroup was hardly the only company concerned about weeding out gunslingers. At a conference at Oxford University in December 2004, Colonel Tim Spicer, chairman of Aegis Defence, and Harry Legge-Bourke, who runs Olive Security, argued that the security industry should be tightly regulated and new restrictions placed on their operations.

Of course, the big companies also had a self-interested motive in doing this, namely, eliminating the competition. The smaller security companies took away huge chunks of the pie. When an industry becomes highly regulated, it drives the smaller firms out because of administrative and compliance costs.

The need for better supervision of contractors has been apparent for years. It is not just a matter of law. There are, actually, quite a few laws and regulations governing the use of contractors. The problem is that there are not enough auditors to monitor contracts.

For example, back in late 2004, the Defense Contract Management Agency went on a hiring spree. It needed 200 civilian employees experienced in overseeing contracts and producing items needed by the military services. The agency wanted people experienced in contract management so they could be deployed to various hot spots, including Iraq, 90 days after they were hired.

Although there were not many contractors involved in Abu Ghraib, I devoted a chapter to it just because it was so notorious.

What does Abu Ghraib tell us about the control over and accountability of PMCs? Though much of the most relevant material is still classified, the bulk of the evidence to date suggests that most of the abuses were carried out by regular military forces. Though several PMC contractors seem guilty of criminal behavior and merit prosecution, it does not appear that the use of translators and interrogators from private firms like Titan and CACI was part of any effort to deliberately avoid oversight. If anything, such efforts came from government agencies like the CIA, which requested the Army to keep certain prisoners off the books, that is, the so-called ghost detainees.

Abu Ghraib, like the overall slipshod, ill-planned way the United States prepared for post-major combat operations, is a reflection of broader policy failings. In short, the Bush administration has tried to fight a war and build a nation on the cheap. It failed to commit the necessary number of trained and qualified personnel and failed to supply the necessary resources required for an occupation force under international law. In such a scenario, failure and criminal behavior by both private and public contractors were virtually inevitable.

The CIA and civilian leadership higher up the chain of command in the U.S. Department of Defense (DoD) created and encouraged the culture in which such offenses occurred. In short, Iraq has shown that higher standards of accountability are required in both the public and private sectors.

In addition, while Abu Ghraib has shown that certain tasks, such as prisoner interrogation, are too sensitive to be outsourced to the private sector without proper government oversight (because of the potential for human rights violations), it is a sad, current reality that the U.S. military plans to continue using PMC personnel for that task because it lacks sufficient qualified personnel of its own.

In the past, some of the primary U.S. laws used to regulate contractors were inadequate. For example, the Arms Export Control Act (AECA) is a key statute in this area, although it is better known for regulating arms sales. The act gives the president full authority to promulgate regulations for this purpose and to designate items as defence articles and defence services by placing them on the United States Munitions List. Any person or organization that manufactures, exports, or imports the goods or services on the list must register with the U.S. government and receive a license for each contract. Criminal penalties can result from a failure to register properly.

But the AECA fails to effectively regulate PMC activities for three basic reasons.

First, it does not provide a mechanism to force presidential compliance. Second, the AECA's reporting requirements provide inadequate information for Congress to assess private military service contracts. However, if legislation passed in 2007 makes it into law that may begin to change. Finally, the AECA provides only limited public information regarding unclassified contracts that may commit the nation to acts of war.

Because the AECA was drafted primarily to regulate one-time arms sales contracts, it does not provide adequate mechanisms for ongoing review of a service contract that may last for months or years.

Moreover, the regulations under the AECA provide no ongoing oversight after an export license has been granted. This lack of public information makes it virtually impossible for the public to assess the practice of private military contracting. Such lack of public accountability would be less bothersome if the regulatory framework guaranteed adequate executive supervision and congressional oversight. But the level of review and inquiry that either branch gives to licensing decisions under the AECA is unclear.

The scarce public information that is available suggests that the current regulatory scheme, while constitutional, does not provide the same safeguards of ongoing executive review, in-depth congressional oversight, and public accountability that is applied to ventures undertaken by the U.S. military. Yet many of the same dangers to American interests are involved when private contractors do the work. The lack of public accountability is perhaps the most important issue because, without it, there is no way for voters to evaluate the adequacy of congressional enforcement provisions or oversight.

It is extremely difficult to generalize about private military and security firms. As an industry, or at least a business sector, PMCs have been around for less than 20 years. And although they have attracted growing attention from analysts, scholars, governments, and the general public in the past decade, there are still no agreements on how to define them, let alone categorize them.

Much of the public image of PMCs is based on perceptions that are woefully out of date, such as the activities of now-defunct groups like Executive Outcomes and Sandline. Specifically, many people still think that companies undertake direct offensive combat operations such as Executive Outcomes did in Angola and Sierra Leone, which is simply not the case. They also think that the various PMCs operating in Iraq constitute a cohesive army, second only in size to the American forces there.

What is worth remembering about PMCs in Iraq is that most of what you think you know is wrong. The private security sector there is very diverse. Yes, there are thousands of Westerners carrying arms, but there are also more host nationals, such as Iraqis and third-country nationals, doing the same. Some PMCs are more low-key than others in using force, but, in general, they are more disciplined and experienced than their active-duty counterparts. And their function varies depending on what the contract calls for. While the common theme for a security contractor is providing security and protection, it can take many different forms, ranging from static security for buildings and infrastructure to security details for officials and reconstruction workers.

The role and impact of private contractors in providing security vary significantly according to context. Obviously, in the case of Iraq, the provision of personal security, primarily for people doing reconstruction work but also for protecting infrastructure, has been the top priority, especially given the dangers caused by the insurgency. This has put groups like DynCorp, Triple Canopy, Erinys, Hart Group, Control Risks, Armoured Group, and Aegis Defence squarely in the public eye.

Though it is not popular to acknowledge it, accountability of and control over private military and security companies have, at least in a few countries, actually been a pressing concern for several years. In South Africa, attempts to regulate have been largely legislative. The problem with South African legislation is that the government views PMC activity with suspicion. Since many South Africans working in this sector had their formative military experience in the apartheid era, the government often viewed them as potential troublemakers, both in other countries and at home.

The United States, in sharp contrast, increasingly views PMCs as part of the total force. Just like the old American Express credit card ad, nowadays, the U.S. military can't leave home without them. Its concerns, bolstered by its experience in Iraq to date, tend to be administrative: how to ensure coordination between theatre commanders and PMCs, how to prosecute PMC personnel if they commit a crime, and how to ensure common standards for issuing and implementing contracts.

Given this, what might be done to improve the situation? The following suggestions merit consideration.

1. Establish an Army-controlled Force Protection Command (FPC) for PSCs. The U.S. Multi-National Force-Iraq (MNF-I) should consolidate PSCs into a unified DoD-backed organization: security companies could be placed directly under the command of a field-grade officer assigned to MNF-I, with appropriate liaison staff big enough to support the needs and operations of all PSCs. This provisional FPC would be assigned the job of organizing, supporting, and regulating all PSC personnel in Iraq and making them accountable under a commissioned military commander.

2. Standardize the entire FPC force. The FPC could transform the PSC world in Iraq into a unified entity instead of dozens of individual companies guarding their own interests and those of their clients. In fact, in Iraq, the principal client is the U.S. government. All security contracts would be managed and contracted by MNF-I, including those of the State Department. Having these contract forces, MNF-I would oversee and be responsible for the protection of all U.S. activities in Iraq. Only companies willing to put their men under the FPC chain of command and meet the Army's standards would be awarded contracts.

3. Dispel the mercenary myth. As long as PSCs operate as commercial entities for commercial reasons of the owners, they will be viewed as mercenaries-mistrusted by U.S. forces and vilified in the press. A strict military command watching over, directing, and integrating with them will help dispel that myth.

4. End the mass contracting of third-country nationals (TCNs). Over time most detractors came to regard PSCs as mercenaries, especially those bringing in large numbers of third-country nationals. TCNs were brought in largely because they would work for low wages and were ethnically distinct from the Iraqis. With the exception of a few companies that

have used ex-British army Gurkhas and United Nations-trained Fijians for years, the recent trend is to strip third world armies of full battalions in order to be the lowest bidder. It lends a bit of truth to accusations that MNF-I is paying foreign mercenaries.

5. Implement strict accountability. The immunity granted to PSCs by Ambassador Bremer's CPA Order 17 should be revoked completely. It should not be expected or welcomed by the private security community. To be able to act with complete impunity encourages rogue individuals and unscrupulous entities to enter Iraq with the intent to "get some and get paid" rather than perform the mission professionally. There have been no prosecutions to date of PSCs involved in questionable shootings or even outright murder. A "What happens in Baghdad, stays in Baghdad" mentality blurs the line between the rogues and the professionals.

Finally, Make PSCs an integral part of the strategy, legally. Congress needs to introduce legislation that would essentially force professionalism and transparency on PSCs. This legislation would also place them in a legally binding framework and protect them under the Geneva Conventions. It should also serve as a reminder that they are being paid to represent the interests of the ultimate paying client, the American people. Of course, amending international law is not done easily, so the sooner this is started, the better.

THE INFAMOUS BLACKWATER SECURITY TEAM

Fallujah, who asked you to come here? (ABC News, 2011). At first, the narrative projected by the media described the dead as non-combatants that did not belong to an army. This gave the impression that the attack was unprovoked and reinforced the Western rhetoric of violent, irrational Arabs. [However, less attention was given to the fact on the 31st of March 2004, various media channels across the world displayed disturbing images of a crowd of Iraqis celebrating the death of two American citizens. The incident which took place in Fallujah, showed two dead bodies hanging from a bridge after being beaten and burned. The crowds, which consisted of men and children, shouted: This is that these individuals were private military contractors employed by Blackwater. Perhaps, their deaths illustrated the realities of a modern nexus of privatized warfare, which demands critical thinking and the need to reframe our narrative of foreign policy and the war in the Middle East.

SOME OF THE BLACKWATER TEAM IN IRAQ

THE CRAZY GANG

Well, the big day came. We had a Hercules plane ready and waiting at Kirkuk to put our whole new office and personal equipment in. I was very impressed. To order a plane like that in a war zone takes some sorting out, so the Yanks mean business down in Basra. It took most of the morning to get our shit together on the plane, but we were ready for wheels up at 2 pm, which was our slot time. We all got in the cargo hold, strapped in, and off we went down the runway. No stopping on to the runway and up and running. We took off at a very steep angle to keep away from rockets, small arms, etc. The journey was uneventful, and I needed a piss. You pissed into a tube. I think that would be the last time I do that, but I was really enjoying myself. MR MOODY, my superintendent, was next to me, and he was creaming himself. He just missed out on Vietnam, so this was his thing. He was loving it and was glad to get out of the bullpen, which was the main office in Kirkuk. We were now a team of 10. We got down to Basra Airport, which was run then by the British Army. We were greeted by a security team and Worly Parson Management team who, unknown to us, had been in Basra for a few weeks sorting out our office, which, once again, was in a camp inside Basra air station, which was a garrison for the British Army. We got to camp, showed our billets, and were told to spend an hour sorting our shite together and meet in the office for a debrief.

We had loads of weapons flying about the place, with security teams coming and going. I thought, "This is it, going to get out of the wire." We all met in the office and were given a rundown on what our job was. It was a mammoth job to undertake in a war zone, let alone peacetime. For the first couple of days, we were just getting our feet under the table. We were still under general order number one, but we were in a Brit camp. We found out there were three bars, one run by the British Army and two underground pubs.

During the first couple of days, we got to meet our security teams. For us, there were three teams consisting of nine bulletproof 4-wheel drives and 27 security lads, mostly English with a few from Australia. We had two days of practice of being shot at and evasive action. If one armored car gets shot up, all good stuff. They gave us all a safety knife to put on our flak jacket. This was to cut your safety belt in case we drop into the many canals on route.

On the second night, the air raid siren went off. Three Chinese-made rockets came in. There was no drama as we were getting used to this stuff. They landed in the middle of the runway.

LIST OF JUST CONTRACTORS LIKE MYSELF WHO DIED IN THE LAST IRAQ WAR UNSUNG HEROES

YOUR LIFE IS LIKE A RAIN DROP AND HOW YOU CHOOSE TO LIVE IT WILL BE OVER AS FAST AS IT ARRIVED SO HOW YOU CHOOSE TO LIVE IT, WILL BE EVERYTHING.

2003

- **April 10, 2003** – American, Robert Grimm, was killed in a vehicle accident on the Kuwait-Iraq border. He was working for the National Response Corp. of Long Island as a fireman.

- **July 10, 2003** – American, name unknown, was killed in a vehicle accident near Basra. He was working for Kellogg, Brown & Root as a truck driver.

- **July 21, 2003** – Briton, Peter Rudolf, drowned when he fell ill while on a dive near Umm Qasr. He was working for Sub-Surface Eng'g as a diver.

- **August 5, 2003** – American, Fred Bryant Jr., was killed by a roadside bomb near Tikrit. He was working for Kellogg, Brown & Root as a truck driver.

- **August 10, 2003** – Nepali, name unknown, was killed by a riot in Basra. He was working as a PMC.

- **August 19, 2003** – American, Nadan Audisho Younadam, was killed in an ambush in Tikrit. He was working for the U.S. Army as a translator.

- **September 3, 2003** – American, Vernon Gaston was killed in an ambush in Baghdad. He was working for Kellogg, Brown & Root as Operations Manager at the Joint Military Mail Terminal at Baghdad Airport.

- **September 4, 2003** – Briton, Ian Rimell, was killed in an ambush near Mosul. He was working for Mines Advisory Group as a bomb disposal expert.

- **September 12, 2003** – Jordanian, name unknown, was killed by friendly fire in Fallujah. He was working for a Jordanian hospital as a PMC.

- **September 25, 2003** – Somali, name unknown, was killed by a bomb in Baghdad. He was working for an "al-Aike" hotel housing journalists from the US television network NBC as a PMC

- **October 9, 2003** – American Kirk von Ackermann was captured on the road between Kirkuk and Tikrit; he is still missing and presumed dead. He was working for IREX Services as a PMC. The CID determined that Von Ackermann died on October 9, 2003, in a botched kidnapping attempt. They still, however, refuse to give out information on his case, which is still "active." Ackermann's body was never found.

- **November 2, 2003** – Two Americans, Roy Buckmaster and David Dyess were killed by a roadside bomb in Fallujah. They were working for EOD Technology, Inc. as bomb disposal experts.

- **November 13, 2003** – American Forrest Snare was killed in an ambush west of Balad. He was working for IAP Worldwide Services as a private contractor.

- **November 17, 2003** – American, Brent McJennett, was killed by a land mine in Tikrit. He was working for Proactive Communications Inc as a communications contractor.

Hungarian, Péter Varga-Balázs, was killed by friendly fire near Ramadi. He was working for ToiFor Kft as a truck driver.

- **November 23, 2003** – Two Americans, Todd Drobnick and Gordon Sinclair, were killed in a vehicle accident between Mosul and Dohuk. They were working for Titan National Security Solutions as translators.

- **November 29, 2003** – Colombian, Jorge Arias Duque, was killed in an ambush in Balad. He was working for Kellogg, Brown & Root as a PMC.

- **November 30, 2003** – Two South Koreans, Man-Soo Kim and Kyung-Hae Kwak, were killed in an ambush south of Tikrit. They were working for Omu Electric Co. as electricians.

- **December 14, 2003** – American, Ryan Manelick, was killed in an ambush in Baghdad. He was working for IREX Services as a PMC.

2004

- **January 5, 2004** – Canadian, Richard Flynn, was killed by a roadside bomb. He was working as a PMC.

- **January 6, 2004** – Two Frenchmen, names unknown, were killed in an ambush in Fallujah. They were working as private contractors.

- **January 14, 2004** – Two Americans, names unknown, were killed in an ambush near Tikrit. They were working for Kellogg, Brown & Root as truck drivers.

- **January 21, 2004** – American Jody Deatherage, was killed in a vehicle accident. He was working for Kellogg, Brown & Root as a truck driver.

- **January 24, 2004** – Pakistani Habibur Rehman, was killed in an ambush. He was working for a Saudi Arabian firm as a truck driver.

- **January 26, 2004** – American, Arthur Linderman Jr., was killed in an ambush near Tikrit. He was working for Kellogg, Brown & Root as a truck driver.

- **January 29, 2004** – South African Francois Strydom, was killed by a suicide bomber in Baghdad. He was working for SAS International as a PMC. Four other South African PMC were injured.

- **February 8, 2004** – Fijian Tomasi Ramatau, was killed in a mortar attack in Baghdad. He was working for Global Risk Strategies Limited as a PMC.

- **February 16, 2004** – American, Ray Parks, was killed in an ambush in Baghdad. He was working for American Services Center as a private contractor.

- **February 23, 2004** – American, Albert Luther Cayton, was killed by a roadside bomb. He was working for Kellogg, Brown & Root as a truck driver.

- **February 29, 2004** – American, Travis B.Whitman, was killed in a vehicle accident in Baghdad. He was working as a PMC.

- **March 16, 2004** – A Dutch and a German, names unknown, were killed in an ambush near Hillah. They were working as water project engineers.

- **March 18, 2004** – Briton, Scott Mounce, was killed by a suicide bomber in Baghdad. He was working for an Italian communications company as a telecommunications engineer.

- **March 22, 2004** – Two Finns, Seppo Haapanen and Jorma Toronen, were killed by a sniper west of Baghdad. They were both businessmen.

- **March 28, 2004** – A Canadian and a Briton, Andy Bradsell and Christopher McDonald, were killed in an ambush in Mosul. They were working for Olive Security as PMC's.

- **March 31, 2004** – Four Americans: Wesley Batalona, Scott Helvenston, Michael Teague and Jerko Zovko, were killed when they were ambushed and massacred in Fallujah; their bodies were mutilated and hanged for public display. They were working for Blackwater Security as PMC's.

- **April 1, 2004** – Czech, Jiří Juran, was killed in an accidental gas explosion at a refinery in Baiji- Iraq. He was working for Chemoprojekt as a petrochemical expert.

- **April 3, 2004** – American, Emad Mikha, was killed in an ambush in Muqdadiyah. He was working for Titan National Security Solutions as a translator.

- **April 6, 2004** – South African, Gray Branfield, was killed during street fighting in Al Kut, his body was mutilated and hanged for public display. He was working for Hart Security Company as a PMC. Bulgarian, Mario Manchev, was killed in an ambush south of Nasiriyah. He was working for SOMAT as a truck driver.

- **April 7, 2004** – Two Germans, Tobias Retterath and Thomas Hafenecker were killed by Iraqi Terrorists in an ambush near Fallujah. They were members of the elite counter-terrorism unit GSG-9 working at the German embassy as guards. The second Officer, Thomas Hafenecker, is still missing today.

- **April 8, 2004** – American, Tim Smith, was killed in an ambush. He was working for Kellogg, Brown & Root as a truck driver. Briton, Michael John Bloss, was killed in an ambush near Hit. He was working for Custer Battles as a PMC.

- **April 9, 2004** – Seven Americans: William Bradley, Timothy Bell, Stephen Hulett, Steven Scott Fisher, Tony Duane Johnson, Jack Montague and Jeffery Parker, were killed when their convoy was ambushed and decimated in Baghdad. Bradley and Bell were initially classified as missing, Bradley's remains were recovered in 2005, while Bell is still missing and presumed dead. Another American, Thomas Hamill, was captured but he escaped the next month. They were working for Kellogg, Brown & Root as truck drivers. Two Nepalis, Ram Bahadur Gurung and Shiva Prasad Lawati, were killed by a land mine in northern Iraq. They were working for Global Risk Strategies Limited as PMC's.

- **April 10, 2004** – American, Nick Berg, was captured in Baghdad and executed on May 7; his remains were recovered the next day. He was a businessman.

- **April 11, 2004** – Dane, Henrik Frandsen, was shot and killed in Baghdad. He was a businessman. Romanian, Aron Alexandru, was killed in an ambush near Baghdad. He was working for Bidepa as a PMC.

- **April 12, 2004** – South African, Hendrik Visagie, died at a U.S. military hospital from wounds received five days earlier in an ambush while escorting a convoy of diplomats from Jordan to Baghdad. He was working for Erinys International as a PMC.

- **April 13, 2004** – Italian, Fabrizio Quattrocchi, was captured, along with three other Italians, and executed the next day. The other three Italians were rescued later that month. He was working as a PMC.

- **April 22, 2004** – South African, Francois de Beer was shot and killed in Baghdad. He was working for Meteoric Tactical Solutions as a PMC.

- **April 25, 2004** – Two Americans, Thomas Carter and Vincent Foster, were killed by a roadside bomb near Baiji. They were working for Cochise Consultancy Inc. as PMC's.

- **April 28, 2004** – Filipino, Rodrigo Reyes, was killed in an ambush in Abdali, near the Kuwait border. He was working for Kellogg, Brown & Root as a truck driver.

- **April 29, 2004** – South African, name unknown, was shot and killed in Basra. He was working for a construction company as a PMC.

- **April 30, 2004** – American, Mike Price, was killed by a roadside bomb near Baiji. He was working for Cochise Consultancy Inc. as a PMC. South African, name unknown, was killed by a land mine in Fallujah. He was working for a British security company as a PMC.

- **May 1, 2004** – American, Christian F.Kilpatrick, was killed in an ambush near Tikrit. He was working for DynCorp International as a PMC. Turk, Cemal Ugar, was killed in an ambush near Baghdad. He was working as a truck driver.

- **May 2, 2004** – Two Fijians, Kelepi Qaranivalu and Emori Vunibokoi, were killed in an ambush in Mosul. They were working for Global Risk Strategies Limited as PMC's.

- **May 3, 2004** – American Aban Elias, was captured in Baghdad, he is still missing and presumed dead. He was working as a civil engineer.

- **May 7, 2004** – American, Daniel Parker, was killed by a roadside bomb in Baghdad. He was working for Kellogg, Brown & Root as a PMC. Poles, Waldemar Milewicz and Mounir Bouamrane were killed in an ambush in Latifiya. They were working as a journalist and cameraman for Polish National TV.

- **May 10, 2004** – A New Zealander, John Robert Tyrrell, and a South African, William (Bill) John Richard, were killed in an ambush in Kirkuk. They were working for an Iraqi construction company as engineers.

- **May 11, 2004** – Filipino, Raymundo Natividad, was killed in a mortar attack near Balad. He was working for Prime Projects International as a warehouseman. Russian Alexei Konorev, was killed in an ambush in Musayyib, south of Baghdad. He was working for InterEnergoServis as a construction worker.

- **May 12, 2004** – Two Turks, Suayip Kaplanli and the other name unknown, were killed in an ambush in Mosul. They were working for Yuksel Construction as construction workers.

- **May 13, 2004** – Two Americans, Henry Doll and Jesse Gentry, were killed in a vehicle accident near Tikrit. They were working for DynCorp International as PMC's.

- **May 14, 2004** – Briton, Brian Tilley, was killed in an ambush. He was working for an Egyptian communications project as a PMC.

- **May 18, 2004** – Briton, Andrew Harries, was killed in an ambush between Mosul and Irbil. He was working for ArmourGroup as a PMC.

- **May 24, 2004** – Two Britons, Mark Carman and Bob Morgan, were killed by a roadside bomb in Baghdad. Carman was working for Control Risks Group as a PMC, while Morgan was working for the British Foreign Office as a petroleum consultant.

- **May 25, 2004** – Two Russians, Viktor Dynkin and Vyacheslav Ovsyannikov, were killed in an ambush south of

Baghdad. They were working for InterEnergoServis as power plant technicians.

- **May 30, 2004** – American, Bruce Tow, was killed in an ambush in Baghdad. He was working for DynCorp International as a PMC.

- **June 2, 2004** – American, Richard Bruce, was killed in a vehicle accident. He was working for Blackwater Security as a PMC.

- **June 5, 2004** – Two Americans, Jarrod Little and Chris Neidrich, and two Poles, Krzysztof Kaskos, Artur Zukowski, were killed in an ambush in Baghdad. They were working for Blackwater Security as PMC's. American, James Gregory Wingate, was killed by a roadside bomb near Haditha. He was working for Kellogg, Brown & Root as a truck driver. Briton, Craig Dickens, was killed in an ambush near Mosul. He was working for ArmourGroup as a PMC.

- **June 11, 2004** – Lebanese, Hussein Ali Alyan, was captured and executed. He was working as a construction worker.

- **June 13, 2004** – American, Shaun Fyfe, died of natural causes. He was working for Environmental Chemical Corp. International as a construction worker.

- **June 14, 2004** – An American, Bill Hoke II, two Britons, Keith Butler and John Poole, a Frenchman, name unknown, and a Filipino, Raul Flores, were killed by a car bomb in Baghdad. The two Britons were working for Olive Security as PMC's, while the rest worked for Granite Services, Inc. as power industry workers. American, Rex G.Sprague III, was killed in an ambush in Baghdad. He worked for Titan National Security Solutions as a PMC.

- **June 17, 2004** – American, Walter J.Zbryski, was killed by a roadside bomb. He was working for Kellogg, Brown & Root as a truck driver. Turk, Faysal Demir, was killed by friendly fire in Baghdad. He was working for a Turkish manufacturer of prefab housing as a truck driver.

- **June 19, 2004** – Portuguese, Roberto Carlos, was killed by a roadside bomb south of Basra. He was working for Al-Atheer as a telecommunications worker.

- **June 22, 2004** – Briton, Julian Davies, was killed in an ambush in Mosul. He was working for Global Risk Strategies Limited as a PMC. South Korean, Kim Sun-il, was captured and executed. He was working for Gana General Trading Co. as a supplier.

- **June 27, 2004** – American, Joseph Arguelles, was killed when his transport plane was fired on over Baghdad. He worked for Readiness Mgmt. Svcs. as an electric power specialist.

- **July 2, 2004** – American, Vern O'Neal Richerson, died at the U.S. military hospital in Landstuhl, Germany, of wounds he received in a mortar attack. He was working for Kellogg, Brown & Root as a construction foreman.

- **July 9, 2004** – Two Turks, names unknown, were killed in an ambush near Samarra. They were working as truck drivers.

- **July 12, 2004** – Turk, name unknown, was killed by a roadside bomb near Baiji. He worked as a truck driver.

- **July 13, 2004** – Bulgarian, Georgi Lazov, was captured and executed in Mosul. He worked for a Bulgarian trucking company as a truck driver.

- **July 17, 2004** – Jordanian, Ayid Nassir, was killed in an ambush in Ramadi. He worked as a truck driver. Turk, Abdulcelil Bayik, was killed in an ambush near Mosul. He worked as a truck driver.

- **July 19, 2004** – American, Mike Copley, was killed in a mortar attack in Samarra. He was working for United Defense Industries as a Bradley fighting vehicle maintenance technician.

- **July 20, 2004** – Russian, Anatoly Korenkov, died at a Moscow hospital of wounds he received in an ambush. He worked for InterEnergoServis as a power plant technician.

- **July 22, 2004** – Bulgarian, Ivaylo Kepov, was captured and executed near Baiji. He was working for a Bulgarian trucking company as a truck driver.

- **July 25, 2004** – Jordanian, Marwan Zuheir Al Rusan, was shot and killed in Mosul. He was a businessman.

- **July 28, 2004** – Two Pakistanis, Raja Azad and Sajad Naeem, were captured and executed. They were working for Al Tamimi group as construction workers.

- **August 1, 2004** – Turk, Murat Yuce, was captured and executed. He was working for Bilintur as a cleaner.

- **August 2, 2004** – Turk, Ferit Nural, was killed in an ambush near Baghdad. He worked as a truck driver.

- **August 4, 2004** – Turk, Osman Alisan, was killed in an ambush near Baghdad. He worked for Ulasli Oil Company as a truck driver.

- **August 10, 2004** – Egyptian, Mohammed Abdel Aal, was captured and executed. He worked as a car mechanic.

- **August 11, 2004** – American, Kevin Rader, was killed in an ambush. He was working for Kellogg, Brown & Root as a truck driver.

- **August 12, 2004** – Indian, Eldho Abraham, was killed by a roadside bomb in Baghdad. He worked for a British construction company "Frame Project International" as an electrical engineer.

- **August 16, 2004** – South African, Herman Pretorius, was killed in an ambush in Mosul. He was working for DynCorp International as a PMC.

- **August 22, 2004** – Indonesian, Fahmi Ahmad, was killed in an ambush in Mosul. He was working for a subcontractor to Siemens as a telecommunications engineer. Turk, name unknown, was killed in an ambush between Tikrit & Kirkuk. He worked for a Tikrit bridge repair firm as a construction worker.

- **August 23, 2004** – Three Macedonians: Dalibor Lazarevski, Dragan Markovikj and Zoran Naskovski, were captured and executed in Baghdad. They were working for Soufan Engineering as construction workers. Jordanian, Beshir Ahmed, was killed in a car hijacking between Tikrit & Baiji. He was a businessman.

- **August 24, 2004** – American, Jamal Tewfik Salman, was captured and executed. He was working as a translator.

- **August 27, 2004** – Egyptian, Jawdee Baker, was shot and killed in Baiji. He was working as a private contractor.

- **August 30, 2004** – 12 Nepalese were captured and executed. Their names were: Prakash Adhikari, Ramesh Khadka, Lalan Singh Koiri, Mangal Bahadur Limbu, Jit Bahadur Thapa Magar, Gyanendra Shrestha, Rajendra Kumar Shrestha, Bodhan Kumar Sah Sudi, Manoj Kumar Thakur, Sanjay Kumar Thakur, Bhekh Bahadur Thapa and Bishnu Hari Thapa. They were working for Morning Star Co. as cooks and cleaners. Three Turks: Majid Mehmet al-Gilami, Yahya Sadr and one name unknown, were captured and executed near Samarra. They were working as truck drivers.

- **September 4, 2004** – American, John N. Mallery, was killed in an ambush in Taji. He was returning to his home base in Baghdad after picking up a payment at Camp Anaconda, Balad, Iraq. At the time of his death he was working for MayDay Supply as a project manager. Egyptian, Nasser Salama, was captured and executed near Baiji. He was working as a private contractor.

- **September 10, 2004** – American, William Earl Bowers, was killed in an ambush near Baghdad. He was working for SEI Group Inc. as an engineer.

- **September 14, 2004** – Two Canadians, Andrew Shmakov and Munir Toma, were killed by a car bomb in Baghdad. They were working as private contractors. American, Todd Engstrom, was killed in an ambush near Balad. He was working for EOD Technology Inc. as a PMC.

- **September 16, 2004** – Two Americans, Eugene Armstrong and Jack Hensley, and a Briton, Kenneth Bigley, were captured in Baghdad. Armstrong was executed on September 20, Hensley was executed the next day and Bigley was executed on October 7. They were working for Gulf Services Co. as engineers.

- **September 21, 2004** – Turk, Akar Besir, was captured and executed. He was working as a truck driver.

- **September 28, 2004** – American, Roger Moffett, was killed by a roadside bomb. He was working for Kellogg, Brown & Root as a truck driver.

- **September 29, 2004** – Briton, Iain Hunter, was killed in a vehicle accident in Tikrit. He was working for ArmourGroup as a PMC.

- **September 30, 2004** – Briton, Alan Wimpenny, was killed by a roadside bomb near Samarra. He was working as a PMC.

- **October 4, 2004** – South African, Johann Hattingh, was killed and one other South African, Gavin Holtzhausen, was wounded by a suicide car-bomber on Sadoon Street, Baghdad. Holtzhausen later died of his injuries.

- **October 11, 2004** – Two Britons, died in Kirkuk, one, Paul Chadwick, accidentally shot himself while the other, name unknown, was killed by a sniper. They were working for ArmourGroup as PMC's. Turk, Maher Kemal, was captured and executed. He was working as a truck driver.

- **October 12, 2004** – Two South Africans, Johan Botha and Louis Campher, were killed in an ambush south of Baghdad. They were working for Omega Risk Solutions as PMC's.

- **October 14, 2004** – Four Americans: Eric Miner, Steve Osborne, John Pinsonneault and Ferdinand Ibabao, were killed by a suicide bomber in Baghdad. They were working for DynCorp International as PMC's. Turk, Ramazan Elbu, was captured and executed. He was working as a truck driver.

- **October 19, 2004** – American, Felipe E.Lugo III, was killed in a mortar attack near Baghdad. He was working for Kellogg, Brown & Root as a labor foreman.

- **October 23, 2004** – Croat, Dalibor Burazović, was killed in an ambush near Mosul. He was working for Eurodelta d.o.o. as a truck driver. Turk, name unknown, was killed in an ambush in Baiji. He was working as a truck driver.

- **October 27, 2004** – American, Travis Schnoor, was killed by a roadside bomb west of Baghdad. He was working for Custer Battle as a PMC.

- **October 29, 2004** – Turk, name unknown, was killed in an ambush in Mosul. He was working as a truck driver.

- **November 2, 2004** – American, Radim Sadeq Mohammed Sadeq, was captured in Baghdad, he is still missing and presumed dead. He was a businessman.

- **November 3, 2004** – American, Jeffery Serrett, was killed in an attack on a prison in Baghdad. He was working for Kellogg, Brown & Root as a medic. Briton, John Barker, was killed by a suicide bomber in Baghdad. He was working for Global Risk Strategies Limited as a PMC.

- **November 5, 2004** – Nepali, Tikaram Gurung, was killed in an ambush. He was working for Gorkha Manpower Company as a PMC.

- **November 7, 2004** – Turk, name unknown, was killed in an ambush in Samarra. He was working as a truck driver.

- **November 8–16, 2004** – A Briton and a Turk, names unknown, were killed during the battle of Mosul. The Briton was working as a PMC, while the Turk was working as a truck driver.

- **November 9, 2004** – Two Americans, Aaron Iversen and David Randolph, were killed in an ambush between Baghdad and Fallujah. They were working for EOD Technology Inc. as PMC's.

- **November 11, 2004** – American, Mike Tatar, was killed with friendly fire on the way to Baghdad from FOB Far ion Huggins. He was working for DynCorp International as a PMC.

- **November 12, 2004** – American, Douglas S.Thomas, was killed by an IED while in a convoy en route to Tikrit. He was working for DynCorp International as a PMC.

- **November 14, 2004** – American, Wolf Weis, was killed in an ambush near Mosul. He was working as a private contractor.

- **November 7, 2004** – A Briton and a South African, Shaun Husband and Johan Terry, were killed by a roadside bomb in Zubayr, near Basra. They were working for Olive Security as PMC's.

- **November 16, 2004** – South Korean, Jung Myeong-nam, was killed in an accident in Irbil. He was working for Taehwa Electric Co. as a private contractor.

- **November, 2004** – South African, Jacques Oosthuize, was killed in an ambush on a road between Tikrit and Mosul. He was working for Erinys Iraq as a PMC.

- **November 25, 2004** – Four Nepalis, names unknown, were killed by a mortar attack in Baghdad. They were working for Global Risk Strategies Limited as PMC's.

- **November 30, 2004** – Honduran, José Mauricio Mena Puerto, was killed in an ambush. He was working for DynCorp International as a medic.

- **December 8, 2004** – Two Americans, Dale Stoffel and Joseph Wemple, were shot and killed outside Baghdad. They were working for CLI USA as construction contractors.

- **December 15, 2004** – Italian, Salvatore Santoro, was shot and killed at an insurgent checkpoint outside Ramadi. He was working as an aid worker.

- **December 20, 2004** – Turk, Saban Ozsagir, was killed in an ambush near Mosul. He was working as a truck driver.

- **December 21, 2004** – Four Americans: Leslie W. Davis, Brett A. Hunter, Allen Smith and Anthony M. Stramiello Jr., were killed by a suicide bomber in Mosul. They were working for Kellogg, Brown & Root as construction foremen and technicians.

2005

- **January 3, 2005** – Three Britons: John Dolman, and Nick Pear, one not known and one American, Tracy Hushin, were killed by a suicide bomber in Baghdad. Dolman and Pears were working for Kroll Security International as PMC's, while the other two worked for BearingPoint Inc. as financial managers.

- **January 16, 2005** – American, name unknown, was killed in an ambush north of Baghdad. He was working for Steele Foundation as a PMC. Egyptian, Ibrahim Mohammed Ismail, was found dead, his body dumped in a street in Ramadi. He was working as a truck driver.

- **January 19, 2005** – Briton, Andrew Whyte, was killed in an ambush south of Baiji. He was working for Janusian Security Risk Mgmt. as a PMC.

- **February 8, 2005** – Croat, Ivan Pavčević, was killed in an ambush near Tikrit. He was working as a truck driver.

- **March 3, 2005** – Two Americans, Jimmy A. Riddle and Brian J. Wagoner, were killed by a roadside bomb in Ashraf. They were working for Special Operations Consulting-Security Mgmt. Group Inc. as PMC's.

- **March 12, 2005** – Two Americans, Jim Cantrell and Bruce Durr, were killed by a roadside bomb in Hilla. They were working for Blackwater Security as PMC's. A Turk, name unknown, was killed by a roadside bomb near Baiji. He was working as a truck driver.

- **March 20, 2005** – Turk, name unknown, was killed in an ambush north of Baiji. He was working as a truck driver.

- **March 25, 2005** – American, Eugene Hyatt, was killed in an accident. He was working for Kellogg, Brown & Root as a carpenter foreman.

- **April 1, 2005** – American, Alfred Habelman, was killed in an ambush. He was working for a California-based construction company as a PMC.

- **April 11, 2005** – Turk, name unknown, was killed by a roadside bomb in Baiji. He was working as a truck driver.

- **April 16, 2005** – Turk, name unknown, was killed by a roadside bomb south of Mosul. He was working as a truck driver.

- **April 18, 2005** – Filipino, Rey Torres, was killed in an ambush in Baghdad. He was working for Qatar International Trading Company as a PMC.

- **April 20, 2005** – An American, an Australian and a Canadian: James Hunt, Chris Ahmelman and Stefan Surette, were killed in an ambush in Baghdad. They were working for Edinburgh Risk Inc. as PMC's. Turk, name unknown, was killed by a roadside bomb in Baghdad. He was working as a truck driver.

- **April 21, 2005** – Six Americans, three Bulgarians and two Fijians were killed when their Mi-8 transport helicopter was shot down near Tarmiya, north of Baghdad. Their names were: Robert Jason Gore, Stephen Matthew McGovern, Jason Obert, David Patterson, Luke Adam Petrik, Eric Smith, Stoyan Anchev, Lyubomir Kostov, Georgi Naydenov, Jim Atalifo and Timoci Lalaqila. The Bulgarians were working as helicopter pilots, while the rest were working for Blackwater Security as PMC's. American, Curtis Hundley, was killed by a roadside bomb near Ramadi. He was working for Blackwater Security as a PMC. Briton, Alan Parkin, was killed by a suicide bomber in Baghdad. He was working for Aegis Defence Services as a PMC.

- **May 1, 2005** – Turk, name unknown, was killed in an ambush north of Baghdad. He was working as a truck driver.

- **May 3, 2005** – Turk, Salih Gulbol, was killed in an ambush near Baghdad. He was working for a Kuwaiti company "Eskiocaklar" as a truck driver.

- **May 7, 2005** – Two Americans, Brandon Thomas and Todd Venette, were killed by a car bomb in Baghdad. They were working for CTU Consulting as PMC's.

- **May 9, 2005** – Four South Africans, names unknown, and one Japanese, Akihiko Saito, were killed when their convoy was ambushed and decimated near Hit. Saito was initially wounded and allegedly captured but died later of his wounds. They were working for Hart Security Company as PMC's under contract to PWC Logitsics at the Abu Ghraib Warehouse Distribution Center near Baghdad International Airport.

- **May 10, 2005** – American, Thomas W.Jaichner, was killed by a sniper in Ramadi. He was working for Blackwater Security as a PMC.

- **May 12, 2005** – American, Reuben Ray Miller, was killed by a roadside bomb. He was working for Kellogg, Brown & Root as a truck driver.

- **May 22, 2005** – Jordanian, Al-Sanie, was killed in an ambush. He was working as a truck driver.

- **May 28, 2005** – Lebanese, name unknown, was killed in a drive-by shooting in Baghdad. He was working as an interpreter.

- **June 2, 2005** – Turk, Salih Gulbol, was killed in an ambush in Baiji. He was working as a truck driver.

- **June 7, 2005** – South African, Séan Ronald Laver, was killed by a roadside bomb in Habbaniya. He was working for Hart Security Companyas as a PMC.

- **June 9, 2005** – Turk, Yusuf Akar, was killed in an ambush in Ramadi. He was working as a truck driver.

- **June 15, 2005** – Bosnian, Ljubiša Aleksić, was killed in an ambush 60 kilometres south of Baghdad. He was working for Lloyd-Owen International as a PMC.

- **June 21, 2005** – Turk, name unknown, was killed in an ambush east of Balad. He was working as a truck driver.

- **June 27, 2005** – American, Deborah Dawn Klecker, was killed by a roadside bomb east of Baghdad. She was working for DynCorp International as a PMC.

- **July 1, 2005** – Turk, name unknown, was killed in an ambush near Baiji. He was working as a truck driver.

- **September 2, 2005**- American Leon "Vince" Kimbrell was killed by a shaped charge IED near the Al-Sadeer Compound in Baghdad. He worked for Dyncorp.

- **September 3, 2005** – American, Ron Wiebe (US Navy Retired RVN Vet), and Briton, Jim Martin, were killed on their way back from Tikrit to Baghdad.

- **September 20, 2005** – Four Americans: Keven Dagit, Sascha Grenner-Case, Christopher Lem and one name unknown, were killed when they were ambushed and massacred in Duluiya, their bodies were mutilated. They were working for Kellogg, Brown & Root as truck drivers.

- **November 12, 2005** – Sudanese, name unknown, was killed in an attack on the Omani embassy in Baghdad. He was working as a private contractor.

- **November 14, 2005** – Two South Africans, Naas Du Preez and Johannes Potgieter, were killed by a roadside bomb on Haifa Street, Baghdad.

- **November 17, 2005** – South African, "Tabs" from 23 Battalion, died as a result of wounds he sustained from a roadside bomb on November 14, on Haifa Street, Baghdad.

- **December 22, 2005** – An American and a South African, Kyle Kaszynski and Jan Strauss, were killed by a roadside bomb north of Baghdad. Kaszynski was working for Croll Management while Strauss was working for DynCorp International. They were both PMC's.

2006

- **January 5, 2006** – Indian, Sibi Kora, was killed by a roadside bomb. He was working as a truck driver

- **March 6, 2006** – South African, Morne Pieterse, was killed by a roadside bomb in Basra.

- **May 7, 2006** – British, Karl Saville was killed in Baghdad. He was working for "Danubia Global" as security contractor.

- **May, 2006** – South African, Richard Andrew Kolver, was killed by a roadside bomb in Baghdad

- **June 8, 2006** – Australian Wayne Schulz was killed when the armoured vehicle in which he was travelling was destroyed by an explosive device. He was working for ArmorGroup.

- **June 11, 2006** - Briton Kenneth Clarke killed in Tikrit by a roadside bomb

- **June 14, 2006** – A Swedish security contractor was killed by an explosive device. He was working for "Genric Ltd.".

- **July 15, 2006** – Syrian, Salih Fawzi al-Madani, was captured in Baghdad, his body was found mutilated at the beginning of August. He was working as a private contractor.

- **August 19, 2006** – South African, Edmund Bruwer, was killed by a roadside bomb.

- **September 17, 2006** – American, Darrell Leroy Wetherbee, was killed by a sniper in Hawijah. He was working for DynCorp as a PMC.

- **October 2, 2006** – Two Turks, Nuri Akceren and Zeki Kilicwho, were killed in an ambush near Mosul. They were working as truck drivers.

- **October 30, 2006** – South African, Morne Pieters, killed by hostile fire.

2007

- **January 7, 2007** – American, Glenda Oliver Butts, died of natural causes. She was working for Two Rivers Consultants as a construction consultant.

- **January 9, 2007** – 2007 Balad aircraft crash, 5 pilots – citizens of Moldavia and 28 Turkish construction workers were killed

- **January 17, 2007** – Croatian Željko Both was killed in an ambush in Baghdad. He was working for "Unity Resources Group" as security contractor. Also, Hungarian, Janos Nemeth, killed same contact.

- **January 23, 2007** – Five Americans: Steve Gernet, Ron Johnson, Art Laguna, Shane Stanfield and Casey Casavant, were killed by insurgents during the rescue of US dignitaries from an ambushed meeting in Eastern Baghdad. They worked for Blackwater and were contracted Dept. of State PMC's.

- **February, 2007** – U.S. citizen Donald E. Tolfree Jr. was killed at Camp Anaconda. He was worked for KBR, Inc. as truck driver

- **February 15, 2007** - South African, Glen Joyce, was killed by an IED in Baghdad.

- **February 18, 2007** - Don Schneider an American civilian driving a post office mail truck from Kuwait to Camp Ceder Iraq died from two 155 round IED's

- **March 2007** – U.S. citizen Carolyn Edwards was killed in Baghdad's Green Zone. She was worked for KBR, Inc. as logistics coordinator

- **April 5, 2007** – Kuwaiti, name unknown, was killed in an ambush in Basra. He was working as a translator.

- **April 15, 2007** – Five Iranians, names unknown, were killed in an ambush in Baqubah. They were working as truck drivers.

- **June 12, 2007** – American, Michael Wayne Butler, was killed by a rocket propelled grenade in Tikrit. He worked for DynCorp International as a PMC.

- **July 15, 2007** – Australians Brendan Hurst and Justin Saint were killed by a rocket propelled grenade in an ambush. They were working for BLP International.

- **August 28, 2007** – South African, Frans Robert Brand, was killed by an IED. He was employed as a security specialist by the London-based ArmorGroup Iraq.

- **October 10, 2007** – U.S. Citizens Michael Doheny; Micah Shaw; Steve Evrard, killed by E.F.P near Al Kut. They was worked as a PSC for SOC-LLC U.S. Private Security Company.

2008

- March 16, 2008 - Briton, Liam Carmichael, was killed when he was thrown from his vehicle after a tyre blow out in Sulaymaniyah, Iraq.

- June 12, 2008 – Briton, Darryl Fern, was killed by a roadside bomb. He was working for AEGIS as a PMC.

- June 13, 2008 – South African Desmond Milnes died from wounds sustained in the same attack as Darryl Fern.

- July 6, 2008- American Justin English was killed when his convoy struck an IED. He was a firefighter for WSI.

- November 13, 2008 – three Russians, two Ukrainians, one Belarusian, names unknown, and one Indian, Jaychandran Appukutten, were killed when their AN12 transport plane crashed near Fallujah. They were working for Falcon Aviation Group as cargo plane operators.

2009

- March 4, 2009 – American, Justin Pope, died of an accidental gunshot wound. He was working for DynCorp International as a PMC

- March 9, 2009 – Pakistani, name unknown, was killed by Katyusha rocket fire in Basra. He was working as a private contractor at Basra International Airport.

- March 26, 2009 – Hungarian, Tibor Bogdan was killed by U.S. soldier near Camp Taji, north of Baghdad

- May 15, 2009 – Briton, name unknown, was killed by a roadside bomb in Hilla. He was working as a PMC.

- May 22, 2009 – American, Jim Kitterman, was stabbed and killed by fellow contractors in the Green Zone in Baghdad. He was working for Janus Construction as an engineer. Larry Eugene Young, was killed in a mortar attack on the Green Zone in Baghdad. He was working for Corporate Training Unlimited as a PMC.

- May 25, 2009 – American, Kenneth Rose was killed by a roadside bomb in Fallujah. He was working as a private contractor.

- May 25, 2009 – Two Americans, Terrance "Terry" Barnich and Dr. Maged Hussein, were killed by an IED outside Fallujah. They were working for the Iraq Transition Assistance Office.

- June 20, 2009 – The bodies of two Britons, Jason Creswell and Jason Swindlehurst, were recovered in Baghdad, they were captured on May 27, 2007. They were working for GardaWorld as PMC's.

- July 17, 2009 – Two Americans, William F. Hinchman and one name unknown, were killed when their helicopter crashed in Baghdad. They were working for Blackwater Security as PMC's.

- July 29, 2009 – The bodies of two Britons, Alec MacLachlan and Alan McMenemy, were recovered in Baghdad, they were captured on May 27, 2007. They were working for GardaWorld as PMC's.

- August 9, 2009 – An Australian and a Briton, Darren Hoare and Paul McGuigan, were killed by a fellow contractor in the Green Zone in Baghdad. They were working for ArmourGroup as PMC's.

- September 1, 2009 – American, Adam Hermanson, was electrocuted in Baghdad. He was working for Triple Canopy as a PMC.

- September 13, 2009 – American, Lucas "Trent" Vinson, was killed by a U.S. soldier at Contingency Operating Base Speicher in Tikrit. He was working for Kellogg, Brown & Root as a private contractor.

2010

- March 10 – Briton, Robbie Napier, an Aegis Security contractor, died after the IED explosion in Iraq

- May 19 – Briton, Nic Crouch was killed by a suicide car bomber in Mosul. Two other western contractors – believed to be Americans – and at least one Iraqi contractor were seriously injured in the attack. All the contractors worked for the British security company Aegis.

- July 22 – Two Ugandans and a Peruvian, names unknown, were working as PMC's who were guarding the U.S. Embassy in Baghdad when they were killed in a rocket attack on the Green Zone.

- September 14 – Briton, Karl Bowen, was killed in a car accident near Kirkuk.

- October 4 – An American contractor, Michael Behr, passed away.

2011

- March 16 – American, Johnnie Lee Smith died in Germany from injuries he received in Iraq when the truck he was driving hit an area covered in oil that had been ignited. He received burn injuries while trying to escape his vehicle. He was KBR truck driver

- June 23 – American, Stephen Everhart, was killed when his convoy was ambushed in Baghdad. He was working for USAID as an "international development and finance expert".

INTRODUCTION

Introduction of striping out and replacing the pumps

Put together while I was in Iraq, the one below is the extraction and the putting back of all the injection pumps in one of the biggest oilfields in the world. If it was not for the local Iraq's this job would not have been completed saying. That you thought the Iraq workforce was on your side, But you did not know which side they went on when it went dark. They could be very nice to you in your face, but you turned your back on them, and a knife could go across your neck; that's why when I was working on-site, I had a team of three all around me tooled up for the job in hand if it kicked off.

Parsons Iraq Joint Venture (PIJV) awarded a contract by Project and Contracting Office (PCO) to rebuild the oil & gas facilities in Southern Iraq.

This Scope includes refurbishing large pumps and synchronous and squirrel-cage induction electric motors, and providing new motor exciter control systems for the synchronous motors. The following is a brief description of condition and work involved.

Below are pictures of some of the pumps we took out and a couple of refurbished ones .

Photos

Figure 2 – Repaired 4 MW Injection Motors and Pumps at CPS 5

Figure 3 – Typical Installation 4 MW Injection Motors - Pumps

Figure 4 – Typical Repaired 4 MW Motor

Figure 5 – Pump House Arrangement at CPS 1. Motors M-1 Thru M-3, Associated Pumps and Auxiliaries Have Been Repaired. Motor M-4 and Associated Pump and Auxiliaries.

Figure 11 – Operating 2.5 MW 2nd Stage Pump and Motor

All those pictures of the pumps were taken out by Iraq locals and transported to um casser, and shipped to weir pumps in Dubai for refurbishment. We found out they were made in Russia but the design was weir pumps. These pumps were put in when the Russians had a stake in Iraq in the 60s. The procedure for taking them out of the pumps was solely written by me. (Weir pumps reversed engineered the pumps and did a perfect job)

STRUGGLE TODAY STRENGH TOMORROW

The reason why we inject water into the oil field

Water is basically injected into a well to maintain pressure.

The Reservoir pressure of Oil Wells naturally decline with age i.e reservoir pressure reduces with time. This in turn affects the Productivity Index (how much barrels of oil you get for every change in pressure). Low PI implies less flow and high PI implies more flow.

Injecting Water into the well helps maintaining the reservoir pressure.

Water Injection method is typically a void replacement method i.e. . injected water replaces the pumped-out oil.

Note that, water is not pumped into the well from which oil is obtained. In fact, a new well is drilled or an old oil well with less production is converted to water injection well.

If a field contains say 5 Platforms, each platform containing 9 wells, then there will be around 5 WI wells for these 45 Wells.

Typically, one can extract only 30% of oil from an oil well, but WI increases that percentage (known as the recovery factor) and maintains the production rate of a reservoir over a longer period. Hope that is explanatory in its simple form.

DON'T DOWNGRADE YOUR DREAMS. MORE IMPORTANTLY YOU CANNOT COME TO YOUR DREAMS WITHOUT FIRST BELIEVING THAT YOUR DREAMS ARE POSSIBLE. LIFE IS SHORT TO BE WORKING ON SOMEONE ELSE'S DREAM, YOU HAVE TO FIND A WAY TO BUILD YOUR OWN DREAM OR SOMEONE WILL HIRE YOU TO BUILD THEIR OWN DREAM.

So we had been in Basra for a week now, and we got intel about the bad guys, what and when they are doing. So Mr. Moody and I decided to go out of the wire to the pump stations and take pictures of the pumps and plant machinery to decide how, what, and how to take these pumps to Weir Pumps in Dubai. We decided with the security team that we should start our missions from tomorrow. Our own security team had been outside the wire most days, planning routes to get to the pumping stations every day, a different route so we did not make a pattern for the bad lads to follow. Extensive areas are still littered with one of the highest densities in the world of unexploded ordinance.

So the next day came, and our team came to give us a debrief of conditions and what to expect. The evening before, we sent an email dictating where we would like to go. We got the ok on that, so it was a goer. Our armoured car was driven by an ex-SAS soldier who had been in the country for six months. The head of the team was in our truck, he was a Brit living in Northern Ireland. He had seen some shit out there when he was in the Ulster regiment. We got on at the outset, so we set off to the edge of the base and loaded our guns at the decimated spot. It took 1 hour to get out of the airbase. We turned right past a load of Iraq tanks with their tops blown off. We were told never to go into a blown-up tank because they use depleted uranium shells. The tanks were radioactive.

Fuck me, really good shit this lot, I thought. Well, on the way we went over the Alshap Waterway. It's where the Tigress and Euphrates meet, and it goes down to the sea at Um Kasa. Mr. Moody asked us to find a safe spot to look over the river to the main lifting pumps that pumped fresh water up to the CPS pumps. I made a fatal error when we found a spot safe enough. We all got out, but only the drivers stopped in the cars. I left my door open, so the driver had to get out and close it. That is a no-no. He has no eyes on the surrounding area, and if attacked, he would be in the open. Nothing was said till we got back to camp, where I had a strip torn off me. But that was that, no malice on both sides. A steep learning course for me. After a few months, I was the best package they ever had (package was me).

So, when we got back on the road and into the desert, we traveled 69 miles to get to one of the CPS. If we went to it in a straight line, it would be 20 miles or, as the Yanks say, klicks. When we arrived, an outer perimeter was formed by the lads. Then, we were told to start our work. We got out and looked at the pump station. It had been shot up with 20mm cannons from warthogs. We discussed how we would take them out. We started taking pictures to look at later and make a report of the said pumping station. By this time, the temperature was getting to 100 degrees. That's fucking hot with your body armor on and steel helmet. We got back into the truck, had some lunch, then moved off to the next CPS, which was around 20 miles away. On the way there, we spotted two cars following us, around a mile away. Every time we turned left or right, they did the same. So, it was decided to cancel the operation and head off home. Once we hit the main road, the bad guys peeled off and went their merry way. We got back to the airbase with no problem. Just inside the wire, we stopped and disarmed all weapons so there would be no false discharges. But a couple of days later, it did occur.

And how it happened, they recruited a new security member who, in turn, was only in the country for one day. Then he came to our team and was given a sidearm, a 9mm revolver. What the twat did was he stood next to the mirror and started to pretend he was having a quick draw with himself, but the silly cunt had a round in the chamber. He pulled the trigger, and the bullet went through all our living quarters (bedrooms), all 10 of them, then exited the dorm where it went, no one knows. He was sent home straight away, never to be heard of again. He could have killed someone, a fucking plonker.

So my feet were well under the table, and at the moment, we would go out of the wire to the pump stations, take pictures, then, when back on camp, write a report on the state of the pumping stations. All good fun. Then at night, we would get mortared on with some type of Chinese rocket. There was once when I was going for a haircut. I was just walking in between two sandbag walls when the siren went off. I thought, "Oh, they will be trying to blow a plane up on the runway when one landed." No more than 40 feet away from me, the sandbags saved me, but it's so funny now looking back. I thought this was normal, so I just said it in passing when I got back to the office. Getting blarza now.

Anyhow, Mr. Moody would not take a drink because of General Order Number One, but that was okay with me, and my drinking did not affect my workload, so both were happy with each other. But there was one day when we, for some reason, were quiet. I think we were in total lockdown because the bad guys were up to something. We had a total lockdown on many occasions and never did find out why, but all good fun.

So, this afternoon, Mr. Moody, who I said before was a Texan through and through, said, "Peter, come into my office. I am going to tell you about the Alamo and not how they portray it in the film." Fuck me; I was in the office for four hours. Not only do I know about the Alamo, but I now know it's a one-star state, and the revenue from the oil goes to Texas, and many other odd things I did not know about. But I listened, knowing when you are marching, you are not fighting, getting paid to hear tosh. Great, as I said before, this is a cash cow, the likes I will never see again. Hundred of thousands of pounds tax-free in 2 years.

Digressing a little bit, on another occasion, I was having a chat with a high-ranking security chap. I forget his name, but he was in the Ulster police/army in the bad times in Ireland. I just asked him how bad were the IRA. Fuck me; he said, "Come into my office, shut the door, and let you into a little secret." He then told me what happened to his pal, who was in the force. He was riding home on his pushbike; he was kidnapped. We found him 4 days later in a sack thrown into a horse trough. When we untied it, his balls were in his mouth, and his mouth was sewn up. When the autopsy was done, he did not drown; he choked on his balls. Then he said, "That's how it was out there."

I left the office, and that played in my head for many days. Then I thought about what these fuckers would do if I was captured. I went outside and had a cigy. So, we were out of the wire most days and spent the afternoons writing reports.

As I said earlier, we were stripping the pumps out and sending them to Dubai. Remember, transporting them to the border was a nightmare to sort out, with it being a war zone. We had to get into a convoy, and we were doing this on a weekly basis. Once we started taking them out, it was decided by top brass to go to Dubai and meet Weir Pumps. So, we planned it for a Thursday till Sunday. We got a plan sorted to get a convoy sorted for early Thursday morning to go to Kuwait, then a plane to Dubai. Off we trotted Thursday, a two-hour drive from Indian country to the border of Kuwait. There was no problem with the bad guys. The border from Iraq to Kuwait is a bottleneck, but we got through pretty quickly. We took off our flak jackets and helmets, put our civvy clothes on, and met the Kuwaiti security team who took us to the airport. We just made it for our plane. We landed in Dubai around lunch, went to the hotel, and met our out-of-country security team.

We did not have the meeting until Saturday, so we knew it was party time in DUBIA on Friday. Our in-country security team took us to this hotel where you pay 50 pounds each, and your drinks are free all day. You can imagine we were like kids with a new toy. It was full of women drinking, but they were not interested in us because they found out we were from Iraq and going back on Sunday morning. They wanted a man who was staying there who they could latch onto for drinks and money. Plus, within two hours, we were wiped out. We got back to our hotel, and I don't know how we got there, but it was only 7 pm. I slept like a baby in clean sheets and took a bath instead of a shower. I woke up around 7 am, ran the bath full to the top, went into the mini-bar, opened two small glasses of gin, and sat in the bath for a good half-hour. Then, I got changed and went for breakfast.

I met the team who all had a bad headache, not just me. At 9 am, we got picked up and went to Weir Pumps for the meeting, which lasted all day. We had a top-class lunch, and then we started the meeting again. We then asked if we shall have to come once a month to see the progress of the pumps, which they said they would fund. Happy days! We finished the meeting, and they took us to this hotel for an evening meal and drinks. We had a good time, but it all ended around 8 pm. We got in a taxi and headed back to our hotel for an early start tomorrow. The plane was at 6 am to Kuwait. The next morning, I got an early call for 3 am, washed, had a pot of tea, and made my way for early breakfast.

We all met at the same time, had breakfast, and got our Dubai security team to take us to the airport. There was no problem at the airport, and we got on the plane. In about an hour, we were in Dubai, where we picked up our Kuwaiti security team who were waiting for us. We reached the Iraqi border and picked up our Iraqi security team, where we were given our flak jackets and helmets. This was it; again, you had to switch off and put your survival head on. We got through the security checkpoints pretty quickly, and then we were in a war zone again. You could not believe that one day we were in a happy place, and now in a shit hole where at any time you could be killed. We got back to base without any problems. We went through the desert, not touching many roads at all. The security teams always found different ways to get home so that the bad guys could not wait for us to ambush us.

TRY TO BE A RAINBOW IN SOMEONES ELSE'S CLOUD

Now, we had been in the country for just over a year. The lad who was the camp boss came down to Basra for a meeting with some catering people for his job on the river. I got talking to him, and I did not know he was selling drugs for weightlifting steroids. He was bringing them in from Thailand, where he was living, and selling them to anyone who needed them. I told him he was a dick, but then he flipped. I found out later he was on them big time. I got to find out that night what a prick he was.

I said to him, "We shall take you to a bar we know," which we did around 7 pm. We stayed till around 11 pm. I was driving, and we got lost. We went round and round; by this time, this knobhead got panicking. Then, the military police stopped us and asked, "What the fuck were we doing driving about on-site?" I told them we were lost, and they told us to follow them and they would take us back to our base, which they did, no problem. So, I thought, but this knob got out, came up to me, and twatted me. I was not expecting that. I was just about to start a fight, but my mate said, "Leave it till tomorrow. You will be arrested and sent home. Remember, this is a cash cow." So, I told him we shall talk tomorrow. We departed in a bad mood.

So, the first thing I did was go to the chow hall to confront this prick. He did not show. I saw him just before he left to go up country, said hi, and reminded him of what he did last night. He said he did not have a clue. So, I sent him on his way, but our paths will meet again when I was on a FOB later on, and how he finished in Bangkok Hilton for 10 years. But that's later.

Well, we were going out of the wire most days, getting info on all the pumps, etc., to be pulled out and revamped. One morning, we went to the big pump house over the river at Qarmat Ali to look at the pumps there to be pulled. We were in for a shock.

Exposure to chromium dichromate dust at Qarmat Ali

During the spring and summer of 2003, about 830 Servicemembers guarded a water treatment facility in the Basra oil fields at Qarmat Ali, Iraq. Servicemembers included National Guard, Reserve, and active duty soldiers and contractors. Many of the Guard/Reserve members were from Indiana, South Carolina, West Virginia, and Oregon.

This facility was contaminated with sodium dichromate dust, which is a source of hexavalent chromium, a chemical that is known to cause cancer.

The Qarmat Ali Water Treatment Facility area was contaminated with sodium dichromate. The chemical was used as an anti-corrosion agent by previous workers at the plant and was found on the ground after bags of the chemical were opened at the site. Those Servicemembers assigned to the Qarmat Ali Water Treatment Facility may have been exposed to toxic hexavalent chromium from breathing contaminated sodium dichromate dust.

The water at Qarmat Ali was not used for drinking, so drinking contaminated water is not considered a significant source of exposure.

Service members who worked in the port at Qarmat Ali or those who simply drove supplies back and forth to the site were at no risk for exposure.

In September 2003, the water treatment plant site grounds were cleaned and covered with asphalt. In October 2003, the U.S. Army assessed the environmental contamination levels and evaluated most of the Servicemembers present at that time. The results indicated low risks for health-related problems for these Servicemembers. However, the amount of exposure of those Servicemembers present *before* the U.S. Army's assessment is uncertain. Therefore, it is difficult to determine an individual's level of risk.

We had been going to this site for a couple of times after the war. I received this below. I thought too fucking late now to get worried.

In response to requests from the Senate Armed Services and Democratic Policy Committees, we reviewed DoD actions regarding the exposure of approximately 1,000 U.S. Army soldiers and U.S. Army civilian employees to sodium dichromate at the Qarmat Ali water treatment plant in 2003. This report discusses the U.S. Army, U.S. Army Corps of Engineers, Combined Forces Land Component Command, and contractor actions from April 2003 to January 2004, specific to the exposure at the Qarmat Ali facility. The team also examined documents totaling over 83,000 pages provided by the U.S. Army Center for Health Promotion and Preventive Medicine, U.S. Army Corps of Engineers, and the on-site contractor, KBR, related to operations at the Qarmat Ali water treatment plant.

We took sworn testimony from 19 individuals assigned to the U.S. Army Corps of Engineers with duty at Qarmat Ali during 2003. We found that DoD military, civilian, and contractor personnel did not effectively address environmental hazards found prior to beginning work to restore to service the water treatment plant at Qarmat Ali, Iraq, in 2003. Preparation was inadequate because contract language describing the site clearance process was impractical. Moreover, the

Army changed the contract scope of work after contractor elements were deployed to Kuwait. As a result, Service members and DoD civilian employees were unintentionally exposed to toxic chemicals and the U.S. Government was made vulnerable to potential health care liabilities for individuals exposed to contamination. Contractor recognition of, and response to, the health hazard represented by sodium dichromate contamination, once identified at the Qarmat Ali facility, was delayed. The delay occurred because KBR did not fully comply with the occupational safety and health standards required by the contract. The DoD response to identified sodium dichromate contamination at the Qarmat Ali facility in 2003 lacked urgency and was incomplete.

So, on the intel we got about Qarmat Ali, we never went back. We just winged it and got the locals to do the study of the pumps. But I do remember wading through the white stuff. The bad guys ripped open the bags, knowing that it would fuck a few of us up over the years. But hey ho, this was a cash cow. Get the money and run.

There was a funny incident in the office one day. I was playing a Beach Boys song, "Surfing USA". I cranked it up and the lads all looked at me. I got up, stood on the desk, and showed them how to surf to the music. Who turned to in the office from Baghdad's big boss was not a happy chappy. I got a big dressing down, and so did my boss for letting it happen. "Do you know we are in a war zone?" Blar blar blar. I thought, grow up, you wanker. You are not out of the wire most days. But hey ho, cash cow.

Well, 12 months in, and we got the nod that on Monday, every pump at all locations should be readily loaded on trucks to join a convoy to Kuwait. Fuck me, that just gave us 6 days. So we worked all day and the next day to get transport up to sites and load pumps onto trucks. Every day, a crane was on-site by a local, and pumps were loaded. By zero hour minus 6 hours, we were done. The next morning, we knew there was a small security team coming up to the first site to escort trucks to the main convoy. So, we loaded up our team and went to the first site. Just behind us was a South African security team. They turned up to escort the trucks. Fuck me; they looked like they came off Mad Max. All suited and booted with homemade armour around the trucks. Armed to fuck, they said while in the country, they had been hit several times with losses. "So now we don't give a fuck. We are tooled up for anything." And to look at them, they were a different breed from our security teams. Anyhow, they signed the papers. Said it would take all day to get them in the big convoy, which would be a mile in length. And that's when they would get hit on the way to Kuwait. This convoy was coming from Baghdad and stopped off near Basra to pick up our trucks. Our job was done. Let them get on with it. We drove home without incident. This is one day in Iraq for convoy duties.

April 5, 2004, Muslim cleric Muqtada al-Sadr called for a jihad against coalition forces, and Thursday night, April 8, his Mahdi Militia dropped eight bridges and over-spans around Camp Scania, thus severing the northbound traffic into the Sunni Triangle. He was hoping to starve the 1st Cavalry Division of fuel and ammunition. Consequently, the 724th Transportation Company was tasked to haul fuel to the north gate of Baghdad Airport from Camp Anaconda, 60 miles away the next morning - Good Friday and the first anniversary of the U.S. capture of Baghdad. Unknown to the truck drivers, elements of the 1st Cavalry Division had pushed militants into the suburbs of Abu Graib, through which the convoy had to travel. Up until this time, the convoy ambushes consisted of four or five insurgents firing on passing convoys with rocket-propelled grenades and small arms. The reaction to enemy contact at the time was to return fire and clear the area.

That morning, five vehicles of the 724th armed with crew-served weapons escorted a convoy of 17 fuel trucks and two bobtail tractors operated by U.S. defense contractor KBR. Enroute, the convoy ran through a well-planned, large-scale ambush that included improvised explosive devices, rocket-propelled grenades and small arms believed to be from one or more of al-Qaeda in Iraq, the Badr Organization, and the Mahdi Army. Convoy commander Lieutenant Matthew Brown was wounded in the head and blacked out, leaving his driver, Private First Class Jeremy Church, to lead the convoy to safety. The attack damaged or destroyed numerous convoy vehicles, and those that made the turn on the overpass drove through the mob of insurgents that had been driven into the neighborhood the day before. Church reached the safety of a dairy factory where a company of tanks waited. He then led a rescue of the stranded trucks and remained in the ambush area when the Humvee he was riding in was full of wounded. Tanks drove the length of the area while scout vehicles recovered Church and Specialist Patrick Pelz. Five civilian contractors and one U.S. Army soldier were killed. PFC Gregory R. Goodrich was killed by small arms fire during an intense firefight for which he received the Bronze Star. Twelve soldiers and four KBR drivers were wounded. Three civilian contractors, Thomas Hamill, Timothy Bell and William Bradley, and U.S. Army soldiers Sergeant Elmer Krause and Private First Class Keith Matthew Maupin, disappeared. Hamill escaped from his captors and was recovered by U.S. forces 27 days later. Bradley's body was recovered in January 2005. Krause's body was recovered on April 23, and Maupin was held captive for an undetermined time before being murdered.

These were the times when no quarter was given. Around this time, I heard that a new superintendent was arriving to take charge of two workover rigs and make a FOB (forward operating base) in the desert. My ears pricked up, and I thought that it sounded a bit scary working and living in the badlands on a FOB. That's for me, I thought, I will have to work on this.

We were still going to the Camels Toe on camp most nights for a couple of pints with the squad, but this came to a halt when they changed the head shed of BASRA from an air force major to an army major. Things changed - no civic in the bar, and he tried to close down the two other bars, but they just went underground. So we went to those after we could not get into the Camels Toe. No big deal, in the great scheme of things, I just had to remember this is a cash cow. Diversifying.

There was an incident when I was going to the barbers when a mortar came down and exploded about 23 feet away from me. I never got hit with shrapnel, and that's when I knew someone was looking after me. I never told anybody. When I got back to the office, they would not believe me, but I did say I was near when it landed.

In Basra, we did not get mortared much at night, but we did get Chinese rockets coming in most days, but they were after planes on the runway. It was the odd time a week we would get one on camp. The food on camp was good - steak in the morning, seafood most days, curry nights, and Asian nights. We did have a good camp boss who had worked all over the Middle East in desert locations and really knew what contractors wanted on camp. He took no shit as well. Up to 2021, he sent everyone a Christmas card. Did not get one after that, may have died, who knows.

Me and Moody got a good banter and work ethic going. The job was going well - still going out of the wire most days. By this time, when going through parts of the desert, there were lakes and ponds starting to appear. They were trying to get the southern marshes back again after Saddam drained them.

The iconic Mesopotamian Marshlands in Iraq, often referred to as the 'Garden of Eden,' also contain the giant Majnoon oil fields. The wetlands were severely damaged by past drainage and warfare. Water availability is still constraining both marshland restoration and the oil industry. We are working with Shell to minimize the negative impacts of oil and gas development on the biodiversity of the marshes and the ecosystem services they provide and to help restore them.

The famous Mesopotamian Marshlands in the lower floodplains of the Euphrates and the Tigris are the largest wetland in the Middle East. The marshes are home to hundreds of thousands of birds and are a stopover point for many migratory birds, including several ducks, pelicans and herons, as they travel from Central Asia to Africa. The marshes are home to more than 200 species of birds and at least 40 fish species. This is also where the Majnoon Oil Field is located: one of the largest oil fields in the world. The word 'majnoon' in Arabic means 'crazy', referring to the excessive amounts of oil. Here Shell (Shell Iraq Petroleum Development – SIPD) is developing a very large project, which overlaps with the only Ramsar Wetland of International Importance in Iraq.

By the year 2000, up to 90% of the marshes were destroyed, and their inhabitants fled, mostly due to the large-scale drainage during the Saddam Hussein regime. In the last few decades, the region has also been the scene of several wars. Mines Extensive areas are still littered with one of the highest densities in the world of unexploded ordinance. Through all of this, only a small part of the marshes on the border with Iran, the Hawizeh Marshes, has remained and is the first Ramsar Wetland of International Importance in Iraq. The other two parts of the marshes were designated as Ramsar sites in 2014.

After the fall of the regime and the end of the wars, around 40-60% of the marshes were reflooded again. A large part of the marshlands, together with three ancient cities, has now been inscribed on UNESCO's World Heritage List.

However, conservation and restoration of these wetlands face serious constraints due to developments, such as agricultural schemes and large dams further upstream, which reduce the availability of water. Solutions need to be found so that the precious river water available is used wisely for the marshes, drinking water and agriculture and that the oil industry does not compete for water or pollute the area.

Map of the marshes

You can waist a whole life time trying to be what is expected of you but you will never be free. May as well go fishing.

Achievements

We worked with Shell to make sure that the oil field developments are taking place with minimal negative impacts on the marshes and the services they provide, and that future developments contribute to the restoration of the marshes by:

- Identification of environmental issues and stakeholders.

- Contribution to the development and review of a Biodiversity Action Plan (BAP), on baseline surveys for biodiversity and the importance for local communities and the regional economy.

- On-going dialogue with Shell on the planning and design of all installations and activities so that they do not affect the marshes.

- Demonstration that re-flooding of currently dried out land can revitalise biodiversity and benefit local communities, and therefore needs to be seriously taken into consideration in future planning of marsh restoration and hazard reduction.

- Identification of further opportunities for marshland restoration, involving the SIPD staff, local communities and authorities.

- For UNEP we carried out a global comparative analysis of the Iraqi Marshlands for biological diversity and institutional management as part of the nomination of the Mesopotamian Marshlands as a World Heritage site.

As I said before, this new job on a FOB was taking off. They were getting a team ready to run the 2 workover rigs and live on the FOB.

I started making inroads to get on the team, like taking the new superintendent of the job out drinking, which he thought was great. We really took to each other, both warriors. He had a word with my boss and he was willing to let me go once it started. He said, "You have done a great job on this project. I hope you do the same on your new adventure." Now it was my job to tie up the loose ends on my project.

The day came when I finished everything I had to do, and I said to my boss, "Going to the new project tomorrow." He said, "Be safe out there on that FOB." And that was it. I went into the other office to start my new job.

By this time it was 4 pm. I got my desk computer sorted, and Steve, my boss, said, "We need a meeting between us two. We shall go to the bar," which we did. So, the new adventure has begun. He said, "I need a camp boss, an electrician, an instrument supervisor, and you. The workforce will be all Iraqis. We have to sort out the company, but he said it's going to be a company called Weatherford from Iraq. They were the best in the game of workover rigs, but our team had to source 2, or should I say I was going to find 2, which I knew nothing about but my boss thought I did. Bullshit again rules, so I had to do some homework."

Reason to perform a workover

Workovers rank among the most complex, difficult and expensive types of good work. They are only performed if the completion of a well is terminally unsuitable for the job at hand. The production tubing may have become damaged due to operational factors like corrosion to the point where well integrity is threatened. Downhole components such as tubing, retrievable downhole safety valves, or electrical submersible pumps may have malfunctioned and need replacement.

Workover Rig doing a Snub Job

In other circumstances, the reason for a workover may not be that the completion itself is in bad condition but that changing reservoir conditions make the former completion unsuitable. For example, a high productivity well may have been completed with 5½" tubing to allow high flow rates (a narrower tubing would have unnecessarily choked the flow). Some years on, declining productivity means the reservoir can no longer support stable flow through this wide bore. This may lead to a workover to replace the 5½" tubing with 4½" tubing. The narrower bore makes for a more stable flow.

Operation

Before any workover, the well must first be killed. Since workovers are long planned in advance, there would be much time to plan the well kill , and so the reverse circulation would be common. The intense nature of this operation often requires no less than the capabilities of a drilling rig.

The workover begins by killing the well then, removing the wellhead and possibly the flow line, then installing a B.O.P commonly known as a blowout preventer, then lifting the tubing hanger from the casing head, thus beginning to pull the completion out of the well. The string will almost always be fixed in place by at least one production packer. If the packer is retrievable, it can be released easily enough and pulled out with the completion string. If it is permanent, then it is common to cut the tubing just above it and pull out the upper portion of the string. If necessary, the packer and the tubing left in the hole can be milled out, though more commonly, the new completion will make use of it by setting a new packer just above it and running new tubing down to the top of the old.

Workovers on casing

Although less exposed to wellbore fluids, casing strings, too, have been known to lose integrity. On occasion, it may be deemed economical to pull and replace it. Because casing strings are cemented in place, this is significantly more difficult and expensive than replacing the completion string. If, in some instances, the casing cannot be removed from the well, it may be necessary to sidetrack the offending area and recomplete, which is also an expensive process. For all but the most productive well, replacing casing would never be economical.

Well got straight into the job the first day in the new office at Basra Air station, but I did not know this job was going to kick me in the arse big time. But that's later on been in Iraq now, over one year and a few hundred thousand better off, so I was hoping to do 2years at least.

So, my first job was to find 2 work over rigs in the middle east, which was harder than you think. The only ones left on the shelf were old and fucked, meaning maintenance was going to be on my shift to keep them running and remember, I was in a war zone in the middle of the desert. If anything broke, it would not be an easy fix, so I had to go out of the country for a week to look at 6 rigs, Dubai, Kuwait and Abu Dhabi.

So I got all my shit together, got security to get me out of Iraq, and started my job. I had an open checkbook. We needed these rigs now, not later. So I went to Kuwait first because it was my first port of call out of Iraq. The company was really a back street affair, all rigs were in bits. I told them I will get back to them. Then, I got a flight to Dubai, booked into a hotel, went down to a bar, got pissed with 2 Brits I met at the bar. They were hired guns just having a drink before going on RR.

I don't remember leaving them, but I think we had a good night. Had a late breakfast and never saw the lads. They must have already gone. So I got a taxi to this factory which was about 18 miles in the desert. They knew I was coming, so by the time I got there, it was lunch. They gave me a belting lunch trying to sway me into having their rigs. I went to look at them and straight away, I knew they were the ones for us. I spent 3 days looking and checking them over, knowing they would need to be working 24/7 for at least one year.

Every night, I sent pictures and notes to my boss in Iraq. He said, "What would be the turnaround to get them to the border of Iraq?" meaning, "Get them to Kuwaiti border so the security team can escort them to the FOB, which was now being built." The Manager said, "From you paying us, we can get them to the border in 2 weeks with all the auxiliary equipment." This meant a small convoy of 10 trucks.

The price was set at $2,000,000. I did not have the authority to do that sort of deal. They would have to wait till I got back.

So, on the last day before flying back to Kuwait, I had another good piss-up. This time, I pissed the bed. Well fucked, knowing full well I was going back to a war zone. Got into Kuwait, no problem, using my KAK KARD as my passport. I was met by a security team who took me to the border to pick up my body armor and kit. Then, I went into no-man's land to meet my team, which I did. In reverse, going out, got to the border, said my goodbyes to the Kuwaiti team, picked my gear up, and strolled around to find my team. There were hundreds of teams at the border waiting for clients or convoys. It was a really man's thing. Everyone tooled up, even me. It was like a Mad Max film. Picked up my team, took the piss out of me for being late, and we might just make it back before dark. You don't want to be traveling in the dark in a war zone.

You will get zapped by the bad guys, so it was suggested we go by road all the way to Basra, not stopping for nothing. If not, we would have to stop the night on the border, but that would fuck up tomorrow's operations for the team. So, I was the package they were taking, me and three armoured cars and 6 security lads told not to go to sleep like normal keep your eyes peeled. This meant we might get EID or be ambushed. I put my safety glasses on; it was one thing I did not mind dying; it was going blind that would fuck me up. Off we set, top speed, and did it in little over an hour. Saw some bad lads over the other side of the road, but by the time they knew we were, we had passed them. The trouble was they had phones, so we went about 2 miles up the rd then into the desert. By the time we got home it was dark, but no mither, good job done.

While the FOB was being constructed, we needed a company to work in the camp, like chefs, cleaners, etc. So we set about interviewing companies from Basra who would fit the bill. We had the interviews in Basra air station. It was a pain to get them in every time; security was tight. These fuckers could bring anything in with them, so they had a security team with them all the time. One of the companies said, "You give us the contract, and we will supply you with drinks and presents for you three". We came to a quick decision; they got the contract, and they had to get their own security to get to the site.

So that was done. The following week, the rigs came. We placed them outside the camp, and we had to put round the clock guard on them. Everything was coming too; the company to run the rigs was given to Weatherford, who used Iraq's. The camp was looking great, made out of hesco bags; big drive up to the gates, the security team was getting their shit together. It was worth millions of dollars, this contract, and at any time, we could fuck it up, but things were going well, and everything was coming together. The day came when the camp was up and running. The 2 workover rigs were in place over the first two wells. Weatherford was on-site, the security team was on site, 150 men and 40 tribesmen looking after the rigs and 5 of us. Great times. We arrived at the FOB around lunchtime. No problems getting there from Basra air station. We went a long way round, and then I saw it - water slowly filling up the desert. They had turned around the water from the Shat Al-Arab waterway from draining to filling up the southern marshes. Below is a little history of the southern marshes.

A wetland in southeast Iraq thought to be the biblical Garden of Eden and almost completely drained during Saddam Hussein's rule, has become a UNESCO world heritage site, Iraqi authorities said on Sunday.

Fed by the Tigris and Euphrates rivers, the marshlands of Mesopotamia are spawning grounds for Gulf fisheries and home to bird species such as the sacred ibis. They also provide a resting spot for thousands of wildfowl migrating between Siberia and Africa.

Saddam Hussein, who accused the region's Marsh Arab inhabitants of treachery during the 1980-1988 war with Iran, dammed and drained the marshes in the 1990s to flush out rebels hiding in the reeds.

After his overthrow by the U.S.-led invasion in 2003, locals wrecked many of the dams to let the water rush back in, and foreign environmental agencies helped breathe life back into the marshes.

The marshes, which covered 9,000 square kilometres (3,500 square miles) in the 1970s, had shrunk to just 760 sq km by 2002 before regaining some 40 percent of the original area by 2005. Iraq has said it aims to recover a total of 6,000 sq km.

Vast, remote and bordering Iran, the marshes have been used in recent years for drugs and arms smuggling, receiving stolen goods and keeping hostages for ransom.

The Marsh Arabs have lived in the wetlands for millennia but are on the fringes of Iraqi society. A study put their population at 400,000 in the 1950s, but several hundred thousand fled Saddam's repression or become economic migrants.

Estimates of the numbers returning vary wildly. Many Marsh Arabs are illiterate and have struggled to find work outside the marshes.

After spending a little while looking at the water now filling the desert, we headed off to the FOB. When we got close, it was fortified by big security gates secured by dog patrols very impressive; we got into camp, found our rooms and spent the day sorting out our office. The head of security came to me and said we have a small problem with the water for the showers. It's dirty and stinks, and you are the man to sort it.

Well, I said, "Where does the water come from?" He said, "The river, every two days and is put into the 2 tanks at the end of camp." I said I would take a look, so off I went thinking this is dog's bollocks. Everywhere I went, brother in arms was playing really great shit. Everyone with a gun strapped to them, I thought, "Yes, this is a man's world." So I get to the tanks, I could not believe my eyes when I opened the top. There were fish in the tank and the water was as it came out of the river. We could catch anything from that shit, so I made a request to have chlorine to arrive more easily than done. It did arrive 2 days later, but it came in buckets with no instructions. So I guessed the first batch. It killed the fish in 10 minutes, which I fished out, and left it at that. One hour later, the security boss came around and said, "I think you have put too much chlorine in the water. Four men have had showers and all have been burnt." So I put a stop to using the shower block until I got new water from the river to dilute the chlorine. Two hours later, a truck arrived and filled up the tanks. Then I was told, "You have a shower first." I said, "No problem, lads," I took a shower and to my amazement, no problems. So, I later halved the dose going in. For a few weeks, I got a lot of stick that it was me who was trying to kill them, not the Iraqis. And you guessed that was my job from now on, but I did not mind. It gave me time to take up the experience of living in a FOB.

We now got an email that the booze was coming in the next shipment of food, so we had to find a secure place for the booze. We took a spare bedroom, put a lock on it, and the five of us had a key to it. The day arrived when the truck arrived with the food, but today there were 2 trucks. The other truck was full of booze; everything you see in a pub, we had it. It took 1 hour to empty the truck with booze. The food truck was second. I wonder why? The food on camp was great. Steak as many times a day as you wanted it. I used to have it for my breakfast. Plus, we had proper bacon, not the Arab shite made out of beef they called "beef bacon"

Now we were getting our shit together; the job was becoming clearer for me. I was bullshitting that I had worked on workover rigs, but it's only nuts and bolts with a bit of angle iron. How wrong I was. We got two teams who would do stag on the rigs 24/7. The security team was helped by the locals on an outer perimeter, for which we paid the chief 100,000 dollars. We would be safe on his land. It was all tribal in Iraq; that's why even now, it's not sorted.

My job was the mechanical engineer responsible for the running of the two rigs. By the time we got our shit together, Weatherford had, with the security team, set up the two rigs over the first two wells to be put online. These were dead wells waiting for the 2-inch tube to go down the 6-inch pipe with attachments on the first tube. When it reached the bottom, they would look at the seismic results from the past to see where the oil was deposited, drop-down belts of explosives to the right levels, and explode them, which would perforate the tube and main pipe. Then they would send acid down, which would open the rocks to let the oil flow up the tube. They would then put a Christmas tree valve on top, bolt it down, open the valve, and flare off the gas and oil for 1 hour. Very impressive, I have got to say.

Every time I went onto the rig, my bodyguard Chris used to come with me. The Iraqi law stated no taking of arms on the rig, but he used to put a 9mm in the back of his trousers just in case it kicked off.

We were now, after a couple of months, doing well every 6 days. You could not get it done any quicker. The oil company was so impressed they bought 2 goats for a celebration feast for us all. The day came when the tribe chiefs, us, and some of Weatherford had an afternoon party with no booze. We were given two goats, and I was given the opportunity to slit one of the goats' throats. Highly honored, I got my knife and slit its throat, but I went a little too far. They said, "Mafi muck crazy English." My name will go down in history out there.

Every other day, we went to see the water coming in from the river. It had been over 8 months since the water started to fill in the marshes, and birdlife and fishes were returning. Please look at how it's doing now after 20 years. I was passionate about it. As I said before, it was as large as the Everglades in America.

We had enough booze to last 12 months. We were given a 60-inch TV from the catering company, plus a paddling pool. That was the start of things going downhill on the FOB. A picture of three of us sat in the pool went to the USA army. Some dick took a picture and put it on his computer. The head sheds sent an email to us to ditch the pond before the army police would come over. As I said before, we were on general order number one and in theater (war zone).

WHAT WAS GENERAL ORDER NUMBER ONE

General Order No. 1 was a general order issued by General Norman Schwarzkopf Jr. to United States Central Command in the Middle East during the Gulf War (Operations Desert Shield and Desert Storm). The order contained provisions restricting the behaviour of troops and was intended to show respect for the laws of Saudi Arabia, where many US troops were deployed. The order, for the first time in the US Army, prohibited the possession, manufacture, sale or consumption of any alcoholic beverage. It also restricted the possession of "sexually explicit" material, which was broadly defined and led to relatively innocuous documents such as underwear catalogs and bodybuilding magazines being banned. A ban on the taking of war trophies from Iraqi prisoners was later amended to permit US troops to retain captured bayonets as souvenirs. The order influenced those issued in later campaigns, many of which also include bans on alcohol consumption even where US troops are not deployed in Muslim countries.

Earlier American troops, such as this marine in Korea in 1951, had been allowed to drink alcohol.

General Order No. 1 prohibited all US personnel from possessing, making, selling or consuming any alcoholic beverage the first time such an order had applied to the US Army. Though this was considered a radical step, it was considered necessary for continued good relations in a country that prohibited alcohol for any of its citizens. Although not its intention, the order led to a reduction in alcohol-related incidents and an improvement in order and discipline among the troops.

The positive benefits of the order led to it being broadly applied to later US operations, whether in Muslim countries or not.

WE WERE PLAYING A DANGEROUS GAME

With the swimming pool incident, things were pretty calm on the camp. All you heard most days in the sleeping quarters was "Brothers in Arms" playing from dawn to dusk. I was going to the rigs most days, which would take 2 hours normally, but in a war zone, it took 6 hours. We used to see the bad guys on the horizon, but they never fired on us. They must have seen how much firepower we had. The lads on the rigs were doing a sterling job, really. If I am realistic, I was just putting pen to paper for my reports. As I have said before, if you have a good team, you look the dog's bollocks to your peers, and it's not you but your team who are making you look good. Remember that as you slide down the barrister of life. Flaring off at night was a sight to see. The desert used to be lit up for 200 yards or so.

CHRISTMAS ON THE FOB

It came to pass that this year it was my turn to work over the Christmas period. My wife Susan knew 4 months earlier that I had to work Christmas, but it was not my first rodeo at not being home for Christmas. I had at least 5 Christmases away from home, but this one I was looking forward to being in theatre (i.e. war zone). I went home in November and came back at the end of the month. We still had to have full security on the FOB with armed guards and dog patrols, so we still had a full crew.

Christmas Eve came and the head of the security team came to my office and said, "Pete, do you want to come with me first thing in the morning before shift change to give the security teams on the 2 rigs a happy Christmas and a swig of whiskey?" I jumped at it and asked what time. "6 am, Pete. I will be on the parade ground ready and waiting," he replied.

We were all ready at 5:45 am. We loaded up and had a convoy of 6 cars. Off we set. We arrived at the outer perimeter with no problem. We then got to the inner security, which were mostly ex-marines and Australians. We got to the main gate, and an old pal was on stag. He was in shorts and a t-shirt. It was freezing. He saluted, and we went through. Nearly everyone was in shorts and t-shirts. We got out, and I bumped into another security ex-marine who I got pal-ly with. I said, "What the fuck's with the t-shirts and shorts?" All he said was, "We are Marines, and we jump into the Arctic Sea." That said it all.

The head of the security team got most of the men together and wished them a Merry Christmas. He gave a speech and then gave me the stage to have my say. I just told them, "These are some times we shall never see again, meaning the dosh we were on." Then I said, "Have a great Christmas!" They all took large amounts of whiskey and saved the rest for the lads on stag. We left and did the same on the other rig. It all took around 4 hours from leaving the FOB to getting back. We had to go back a different way because of the bad guys who could turn up.

So back on the FOB, I thought, "Christmas now." I went to our hooch with the booze, took a bottle of Gordon's gin, went to my room, and started playing music. "Brothers in Arms" was echoing all over the camp. I thought, "This is awesome, I will never have these times ever again, men amongst men." I went into the canteen for lunch, and they did a great spread from turkey to lobster. I had a great feed and the crack.

So, Christmas came and went. January came and went. I was still sorting out the engineering side of the rigs with no problems, as well as the maintenance of the water pumps in the camp. I still got ribbing from the lads about how I burnt some of them with the chlorine I put into the water. FOB life was very mundane. I used to write my daily reports a day before and just add anything else that cropped up.

To pass the time, I used to go to the kennels and play with the sniffer dogs. It was great fun. Going on leave was a pain in the arse. You had to book your flight from Kuwait, then arrange to get back to Basra, and from Basra to Kuwait. But by this time, we had a Russian Antonov which we hired for 2 days a week. The other times, it was smuggling God knows what from Africa. This plane had worn tires down to the canvas and a fucking motley crew, but they were the only outfit that would fly into Iraq. Landing was a fucking art from 10,000 feet to landing in about one minute. It was very scary.

WAS THIS THE PLANE WE FLEW ON

The 2007 Balad aircraft crash was an airplane incident involving an Antonov An-26 airliner, which crashed on 9 January 2007 while attempting to land at the Joint Base Balad in Balad, Iraq, which was at that time operated by the United States Air Force. The crash killed 34 people aboard and left one passenger critically injured. Officials claim the crash was caused by poor weather conditions, but other sources claim that this is a cover-up and the plane was actually shot down by a missile. WHO KNOWS, AND WHO CARES.

THE PURPOSE OF OUR LIFE IS TO BE HAPPY.

By this time, I had been on the FOB for about a year, and things were just ticking by. However, unknown to me, the camp boss, who was the twat that threw a punch at me in Basra air station, was supplying some of the security teams with muscle-building pills, etc. This was a dangerous game to be playing with the AMERICAN ARMY, which we were attached to, and being on General Order Number One. I was getting some feedback from the lads at Basra that we were running a fucking holiday camp. "Watch your backs," we were told. Not thinking much of it, I thought they were jealous of us being out here.

So what happened next got 10 or more people sacked, and one full bird colonel was put on home arrest and could lose his pension. It was time for my superintendent and me to go on RR. We got all our shit together, and we were flying out of Basra on the ANTIHOFF with bald tires. We left the FOB at 0500, and the camp boss was in charge of the camp, not the security team, just the camp. So we headed off. It took us around two hours to get to Basra over the desert, missing any roads and built-up areas. We got to Basra and went for a debrief. I could smell that something was not as rosy as it was last time, but I thought nothing of it. Our plane was taking off at 2 pm to Kuwait, then another plane to London, then Manchester. But your leave started when you took off from Basra, so you did not get three weeks. It was short of three, but paying us big bucks, who gives a shit.

Came home, had a week's holiday in Spain with Sue, got pissed, and before you know it, it's time to go back. Some of the lads back home were saying, "You must be fucking mad going back there." I just smiled and just thought of the money. It never ever bothered me about dying, being wounded, just going blind pissed me off a bit. I always, when out of the wire, had safety glasses on. There was one other thing, drowning in one of our trucks a year earlier. One security team's car went into a flowing stream, turned over on its side. The doors are that heavy, you just cannot open it; it needs at least two of you. When it's on your side, with bulletproof glass, you can smash it by hitting it in the corner; it's made that way. Every truck had a sledgehammer for that, but this time they smashed the front window, which brought all the water in. One guy was stuck in his seat belt before a knife was taken to cut the seat belt. He panicked and drowned. I had nightmares for months after that. I always carried the tool, like a knife, in my flak jacket. At least I could cut myself out if needed.

So on me leaving Susan and playing "Leaving on a Jet Plane" for the last time, I got in the taxi and off to the airport. After 10 minutes of getting into the taxi, my head was back on a war footing. No drama getting back into theatre, as they called it, but I heard a whisper waiting for the plane to take us to Iraq. Something has been going on. I thought I best not say owt, just play mum.

SHOW ME YOUR FRIENDS AND I WILL SHOW YOU YOUR LIFE. HANG OUT WITH LOSERS YOU WILL FINISH UP AS A LOSER.

By the time I got to the air base and was picked up off the plane, I knew that the shit had hit the fan. I was summoned to the big boss, who greeted me sheepishly. Then he started asking, "What the fuck have you been doing on the FOB for 6 months? I know you did your job, but what was going on in the FOB? As you're aware, you were on general order number one." I said, "Yes, I know. So what has been happening?" I thought to myself, "Keep being the grey man. Don't want to drop myself in the shit. And if they had anything on me, I would be arrested by now by the military police."

Well, he started to explain that the camp boss had gotten four security guards pissed, and one other full-bird colonel was under house arrest in Baghdad for allegedly being there.

The 5 of them were now back home, thrown out of the country. A bit bad when in a war zone. So what happened was there were 6 of them, the colonel left. The rest got pissed on the free booze, then the camp boss got the drugs and booze in his system. Then he did what he did to me 12 months earlier, twatted one of the guys, which was not a good thing. Being an ex-marine, he no more floored him and gave him a good kicking, but this was not all. When the party had finished, this twat got up, woke the commanding officer, wanting these four to be sent home. Now this was 3 o'clock in the morning, remember we were 60 miles away in the bad lands. You just cannot get a truck and take them to Basra. So the head shed tried to calm the situation down but got no joy. So he got in touch with Basra, got clearance to bring these 4 lads in, was told by the American army everyone involved had to come back, even the colonel had been mentioned. He was dragged out of bed, so they made up a convoy and sent them to Basra. Meantime, the rest of the lads on the FOB started pouring the drink we had stashed down the drain. Next day, they were all sacked on the spot but not the colonel because he was AMERICAN ex-army. He could lose his pension. He was taken to Baghdad and put on open arrest. He could not use his computer, it was taken away for checking. Now my computer, my bosses computer, we're being checked over, my boss who now was in another room being quizzed, and all computers on site were being checked to see if any pictures of people drinking. And if they found any and could say it was in Iraq, they were sacked on the spot. He did say 10 have been sent home, but we cannot find one of you. The reason being, I would not have anybody take a picture of me with a drink in my hand. I had learned a lot over the years, try to be the grey man.

So he then said, "Your boss has a picture of him with a drink so he is going home today. He then said, "You are not going back to the FOB; you are going back to the main office to work there. This will go on your record, but I can not prove you were part of this so you will be watched all the time while in Iraq."

As I was leaving, he did say, "You live a charmed life Oldham, If you ever write a book the fucking paddling pool has got to go in." And, "Oh, we found some very expensive golf clubs." I said, "Not mine, don't play golf." Then he just said, "Fuck off, and I don't want to see you again on this side of the table." I left the office thinking that it was close.

Now, there is another turn here. The camp boss got repatriated to Thailand, where he had a house and a Thai woman. A few months later, the woman found he was shagging another woman. She only went to the police and told them what he was selling, and he was arrested and did 10 years in Bangkok Hilton. Karma comes into play here.

So, I went to see the boss in the office. He just laughed and told me I was going to work with Mr. Moody again on the pumps which we took out last year, and they were ready to be installed.

So, I thought I got off pretty lightly, but it was not the same in the office. People had gone, and the people who were here were all trying to get up the ladder. Me and Moody did our own thing. Basra Air Station had been taken over by the British Army general. Before, it was a Royal Air Force general who was a bit lax. I did one night try to get into the Camel's Toe, but was told it was closed for contractors. So, I then went to the illicit bar where, if I was caught, they would throw the keys away. But I said, "Fuck it. Got the t-shirt. Not many people have done what I have done and seen." I had been there nearly 2 years, 4 weeks, and it would be 2 years in a war zone and out of the wire most days more times than the average contractor many never left camp I enjoyed every minute out of the wire because I had the best professional security.

Teams looking after me my hat goes off to them and a very big thank you to them all. There was one thing I had to do, which was to tell the American government that the guy they had on open arrest was only there for the first hour before they started drinking, and he was a teetotaller.

So I did some prying and found his colonel-in-chief. I sent him an email that was 3 pages long, explaining how he was a Christian and a

Methodist, etc. It must have worked. Two weeks later, he was home in the USA. He sent me an email thanking me for what I had done and said he would repay me. I thought that was good. He got his pension and a clean slate. Now, two weeks later, I got a funny email from a company in America. It said I had been selected for a position with them. I would get a green card, and my family would be able to move to America. I had one week to decide. I thought, "What the fuck?" I have now forgotten the company, but "the Skunk Works" rings a bell. Please look up the Skunk Works. Anyhow, I showed it to Jim, my boss. He said, "How the fuck did you get this? I have been trying for years. You have got to go." But he said no more. He had a word with Susan. She was not happy about moving to the USA, so I left it for over a week and thought, "Fuck it, I am going. If Susan does not want to go, she can stay in England." I sent the email, but I never got a reply because Susan would not live in the USA. I am sure that another week later, I emailed them again but got nothing. It got pinged back. Years later, I asked Jim what the company was that had offered me the job in America. He said, "I cannot say, but you should have taken it." So who knows? Now, another funny thing happened a week before I was going on leave, which would have been 2 years and one month. My contract was terminated. I wonder why. They have spooks in the USA army; they know all the traffic on your computer. Did they see who I was emailing about the job? I will never know. So the day came to leave. I am not a man for saying goodbyes. I choked up a bit, so I left at the last minute. I said no goodbyes. I left as I came in, a nobody, just a grey man who had a great time. On the last note, when I was 60, my wife got in touch with the head security, who was still out there, and asked if he had something he could send for my 60th birthday. He came on leave and sent Susan my pot helmet with my name on it. He found it, and in the letter, he said they were after Peter, but they could not find any picture with a drink in his hand. Fare play to him. So, I came home one April. I never really came down from that high, and I still miss the comradeship, men amongst men.

I CAME I SAW, AND I CONQURED

Well, I grovelled back to my old job in the UK building the DSB. As I told you, the job was okay, but I did not get the buzz really. So, three years down the line, I was asked if I would like a short stint in Iraq. It sounded like they were in deep shit, so I said yes. The money was not as good because it was now just the odd bombs and kidnappings, but it was still good. So, I told the firm I was going. The big boss said, "You will never come back here again," but I wanted the adventure. So, I left Susan once again on a wet and dreary Tuesday morning, and yes, the last thing I played was "Going on a Jet Plane".

I got to the airport and got my Iraq head on. We arrived in Kuwait, no problem. Then we boarded a plane to Basra. The airport was trying to get back to normality, but still a long way to go. We went through customs, no problem. Then, I met my security team. Fuck me, just boys, not like in the good old days when it was survival. Now, it was just a walk in the park. We got to the main office and met a few of the team. We then went for security passes. By this time in Basra air station, the Brits had gone, and the Yanks with cheap security from Africa, a right rag-tag and bobtail lot. So, we had an eye scan, which I was told, "You are now a marked man all over the world. You cannot go anywhere we cannot find you." That was interesting, but the Yanks looked like they were a 2nd class of soldier, but did not worry me, getting paid tax-free.

So, we got that done, loaded up and went to our digs on a FOB which was shite. We were told we had to collect all the data on the pumps, vessels, etc., from 8 different sites so they could put in a price for the work. But we found out we had only 5 weeks to do it in. Fucking impossible! Below is a report of one of the sites which were spread all over the desert.

MUSHRIF QURAINET

We did comprehensive and progressive record-keeping for each pump, compressor, and generator, detailing components and procedures, preventive maintenance intervals, operations, and operational issues. A maintenance routine should be planned with the service conditions in mind, rather than as an arbitrary routine or only when the equipment malfunctions or a reduction of flow or performance can be determined fairly early by continuous monitoring of equipment and their records.

This site is in excellent condition with only small mechanical problems. This was the type of everyday report we had to do. One site was full of vessels, and I had to take UT readings to measure the thickness of the vessel. I got there and, as I was writing down the nameplate, they were built in the 60s in Hyde, where I come from Joseph Adamson, and they were still going, and no corrosion. That was engineering for you. They don't make steel like that any more.

So we were working flat out 12 hours, 7 days a week, and it still was not good enough for them. I said to the lads, "Fuck this. Where are we?" We got emails saying they were bringing in another group to help us. I said to the lads again, "No, they are getting rid of us," and yes, a month later, I was told my contract was finished. I was not bothered. By this time, I had enough of the bullshit. It was not a war zone anymore, just a bitching match between oil companies over who was going to get what, and we were in the middle of it. Time to go.

I returned home and asked for my job back, which I got back once again.

***

I am now retired and have had a rollercoaster of a life, but I wouldn't change a single thing. Perhaps I could have moderated my drinking a bit, but that does not make me a bad person. Susan, my dear wife, has put up with a lot from my exploits, and she was the stabilising force in my life. We are now stronger than ever before and are fully enjoying life by doing what we want, rather than what others tell us to do. You too can reach this level of contentment. Be strong, push a little harder, and think outside the box. You are a child of the universe, no less than the trees and the stars.

Declassifiey

***

www.ingramcontent.com/pod-product-compliance
Lightning Source LLC
Chambersburg PA
CBHW030038100526
44590CB00011B/249